C000185978

Ahead of the

The Marketing Guide
for Small Business

This book was won
by 'Nox' 2003 / 2004,
dedicated to future
Young Enterprise companies.
Enjoy!

Ahead of the Game

The Marketing Guide
for Small Business

Lynn Moffat

The McGraw-Hill Companies

London   Burr Ridge, IL   New York   St Louis   San Francisco   Auckland   Bogotá
Caracas   Lisbon   Madrid   Mexico   Milan   Montreal   New Delhi   Panama   Paris
San Juan   São Paulo   Singapore   Sydney   Tokyo   Toronto

Published by
McGraw-Hill Publishing Company
Shoppenhangers Road, Maidenhead, Berkshire, SL6 2QL
Telephone: +44 (0) 1628 502 500
Fax: +44 (0) 1628 770 224
Website: www.mcgraw-hill.co.uk

Sponsoring Editor: Elizabeth Robinson
Editorial Assistant: Sarah Wilks
Production Editorial Manager: Penny Grose

Produced for McGraw-Hill by Steven Gardiner Ltd
Printed and bound in Great Britain by Bell and Bain Ltd, Glasgow
Cover design by Senate Design Ltd

McGraw-Hill

A Division of The McGraw-Hill Companies

British Library Cataloguing in Publication Data
A catalogue record for this book is available from the British Library

Library of Congress Cataloguing in Publication Data
The Library of Congress data for this book is available from the Library of Congress

ISBN 0 07 709839 0

McGraw-Hill books are available at special quantity discounts. Please contact the Corporate Sales Executive at the above address.

With thanks

Thank you to everyone who helped, especially as the stressful deadlines loomed – some things never change!

Particular thanks to Simon – the man with little patience – the greatest compliment was for him to tell me he didn't want to stop reading the book.

Thanks to Mark, Alison and in particular Andy Bryce for his feedback and reassurances.

And thanks to my family for making me proud to see them get on with their small business in the most difficult of times.

Contents

Introduction

Whenever you see a successful business,
someone once made a courageous decision.
Peter Drucker

Have you ever found yourself in a position like this:

- You long for freedom and control. You have a vision and feel that with your brilliant idea you just can't wait any longer. Imagine how you'd feel if someone else stole a march on you and started a business doing what you saw as your great opportunity.
- You've always wanted to be the boss. Perhaps your company has hacked you off for the last time. You want to control how the job is done.
- You're steeling yourself for a brave leap into the unknown because you feel if you don't do it now you never will.
- People keep telling you you're so good at what you do you should be doing it for yourself.
- You want to do a job you really love – something you've always wanted to do – for yourself.

Driven to it or going for it – it doesn't matter. You've decided that now is the time to 'go it alone' – totally alone or with a handful of colleagues – but certainly without the 'security' of a regular monthly income, controlling boss, Monday morning blues, company politics and watching others get the glory!

You are now officially a Small Business: congratulations! You are now in charge.

What you are is an individual with a great idea and the guts to try to make it work. What this book aims to do is give you guidance on things you *must* or *should* do to get and keep hold of customers, stay ahead of the game and make sure your idea succeeds.

Many of you started your business with great ambitions of growing it into a large and valuable organisation. But not everyone wants to grow their small business – why should they if they are happy with the satisfaction that simply running their operation brings? My aunt is a fabulous florist who always wanted her own business. After years of working for others she took the plunge. Now she's running her business, she has no intention of turning it into a huge chain of shops with people and administration issues to manage. She loves being a florist – she's passionate – she wants her outlet to be profitable and successful for sure – but she doesn't plan for growth and expansion. If the business grows, great – but that's not her reason for being.

Either goal is of course absolutely fine: it's down to the individual. This book has been written for any ambition. My assumption is not that everyone wants to become a huge company, but that everyone wants their business to be as successful as they want it to be. One that will reward them with sufficient return to satisfy themselves (and of course any bank or body who has a financial interest in the venture).

Did you leave a large organisation behind? (Maybe that's where you'd like it to stay – a dim and distant memory for one reason or another.) Please don't forget about such experiences: as a small business you are in a great position to look at large companies (those for whom you worked or were customer of) and learn from what they do well and badly, to customers and staff. With no rules or strict procedures in place, able to be much more flexible and responsive, much closer to and knowing more about customers, you are in a position any large company would kill for. This book will not ask you to be like a large organisation, but it will ask you to use some of the thinking that makes them successful, and avoid the things they do badly.

What I want is for this book to be an antidote to all those business books out there that seem to be written for the company with millions to spend and a staff of hundreds of people. You may not be surrounded by a team of people who have MBAs or marketing and business experience. You probably don't have time or money at this stage to discuss, research and analyse before the 'team' make a decision. It is meant to provide a practical, realistic, simple and honest approach to getting your business going – marketing it if you like. And once it's up and running it presents some ideas to keep it going successfully – things you might want to consider adopting so you stay ahead of the game.

In writing this, I am assuming that you have done a lot of the hard work required to get up and running – getting money together, finding an accountant and solicitor, taken advice from any bank or small business advisors, and set up your business as either a sole trader, partnership or limited company. This book is not about the administrative side of your small business, although if you haven't got funding yet you might find it of help in preparing a detailed business plan – demonstrating to others (and reinforcing to yourself) exactly what you aim to do, how you aim to do it and why you'll be successful.

I found it quite hard to put all the ideas into discrete chapters. Your customers are not going to think in such a structured piece-by-piece manner. Nor when you are applying the thinking of one chapter can you act in isolation from other chapters. However, I have tried to make it as user friendly as possible. The structure is designed to allow you to search for ideas, examples and current thinking in specific areas which may concern or interest you. By the end of the book, having read each chapter, you should have an idea of how to integrate all the thinking into a great offer – one that finds customers and keeps them coming back to you time and again.

The first three chapters look in general terms at what it means to stay 'ahead of the game' and what marketing your business really involves. The remaining chapters get into the specifics of where to stay ahead and how to stay ahead – how to market your business successfully.

Please let me know what you think – tell me how the ideas in the book have been helpful. If you want to pass on to me examples of your applied wisdom that I can include in the next edition, then please do so.

I

What Marketing Is All About

(and what it's not about)

THE CHAPTER AT A GLANCE

Being great at marketing will help you get and stay ahead of the game.

Being a marketing-oriented business will increase your chances of success. What is marketing, if it can be so important to the success of your business?

Chapter 1 talks generally about these things – what we mean by marketing, what it is and what it isn't. Why it is so important. Why it can help you stay ahead of the game and how it can help do it

WHAT YOU THINK MARKETING MEANS

What I'd like you to do first is to think about what the word 'marketing' means to you. Think about all the things you and your company do that is 'marketing'. What about your competitors? Think, too, about any companies you think are really good at marketing, no matter how big they are or what sort of business they are in.

What did you come up with? Advertising? Selling? Sending out brochures? Having a page on the Internet? Arranging a stand at an exhibition? Doing some market research? Absolutely right. All these things are marketing. But they are marketing in its narrowest sense. What these tasks represent are the jobs people do, or what the people you call marketers do, or what you do to try to drum up business when you need it. Absolutely no doubt, all essential things – these are marketing tactics.

But marketing is much more than just tactics

What we're going to look at is the broad concept of marketing. Marketing in its entirety. Marketing as an orientation, an approach to everything you do in your business. How you can use this marketing approach in your small business. Why you will be successful using this marketing approach across everything you do.

Think about the advertising, selling, brochures, exhibition stands and other such tactics as the tip of the iceberg or the icing on the cake. Unless there is something beneath the surface holding the iceberg up it won't last very long. Unless the partygoers like the taste of the cake beneath the icing then you don't have a successful cake. You can spend your hard-earned budget on printing as many glossy brochures as you want, but unless the actual content of what you are offering for sale is right then the brochures are a waste of

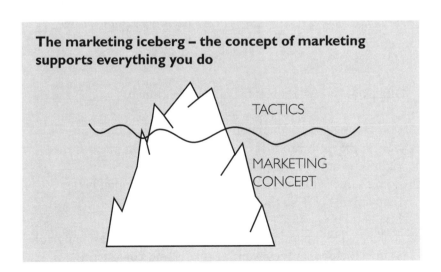

The marketing iceberg – the concept of marketing supports everything you do

TACTICS

MARKETING CONCEPT

money and time. The marketing concept has to run through every part of your business, supporting everything else you do – and be a solid base for your tactics.

So exactly what do we mean by the marketing concept?

A DEFINITION OF MARKETING

In your definitions of marketing, many of you have perhaps mentioned the broader marketing approach, the supporting part of the iceberg beneath the surface. So what is it all about? It's hard to come up with one definitive answer to the question. The following quotations give just three of the many different definitions by marketing gurus.

the key to achieving organisational goals [by] determining the needs and wants of target markets and delivering the desired satisfactions more effectively and efficiently than competitors.

Philip Kotler[1]

Marketing involves every employee in building superior customer value very effectively for above-average profits.

Hugh Davidson[2]

A management process responsible for identifying, anticipating and satisfying customer requirements profitably.

Chartered Institute of Marketing

Other phrases which you may have mentioned:

■ doing things better than competitors
■ having the right product or service in the right place at the right time at the right price
■ doing something that customers really want, much better than anyone else, so those customers choose to come to you first
■ making sure you are the supplier a customer sees as being able to give them what they want, regularly and consistently

■ satisfying a customer so much that they return to you time and time again, recommend you to friends, feel they have a relationship with you
■ a process of building customer loyalty by being the best
■ being customer oriented – striving for customer satisfaction in everything you do
■ having an advantage over competitors when it comes to satisfying specific customer needs
■ identifying customer needs and using your skills and resources to satisfy these particular needs better than anyone else can, and in return generating above average return for your business.

All are part of an acceptable definition.

The last one in the list above comes closest, for me, to capture all the required elements so this will be the definition I offer.

Marketing is a process of identifying customer needs and using your skills and resources to satisfy them, profitably and better than competitors.

If marketing is about satisfying customers then this alone should convince you that marketing is not just the advertising or brochures – your whole company is about marketing. Customer dissatisfaction can come from anywhere and anyone and anything in your business: the price to pay, the level of price increases over last year, the delivery standards, the quality of the workmanship, the length of time taken to complete a job, the manner of a telephone operator and so forth.

So step 1 in being a marketing-focused business is to make sure everyone who works with you knows this – *everything* your business does revolves around satisfying your customers. Everyone does what they do in order to satisfy customers.

This in itself sounds easy, yes? Give people what they want and satisfy them at every turn. The problem is that customers, if they had the choice, want better and better products and services for free! So marketing is actually harder than it sounds – it's about satisfying customers while at the same time ensuring you make an adequate return: a better than average profit. It's about satisfying customers while at the same time doing it better than your competitors, the large companies and businesses like yours who are trying to capture the money the customers have to spend – competing for a share of the mind – trying to convince customers to abandon you and go with them. I's about satisfying customers by trying to identify the real needs driving their requirements. Which customer needs do Rolex watches satisfy? The need to tell the time accurately, the need to have the best Swiss timepiece, or the need to demonstrate wealth and prestige to others? Chapter 2 explores more fully the customer needs you are satisfying.

If your business embraces the marketing concept as a driver of all you do, it gives a strong foundation on which to base your tactics. If your business is founded on the definition of marketing, your tactics are more likely to be well thought through and targeted.

THE REASON FOR MARKETING

Some people think that marketing is an expense. The frills and icing such as advertising may be, but again that's the concept in its narrowest sense. The reason for marketing is simply and clearly to ensure that you, as a small business, remain profitable in the long term.

When times in the economy and in your industry are good then you don't need to be that great as a business in order to be profitable – there's so much custom around that you can just go in, get the job done and leave for the next one. Think about builders and decorators and estate agents as examples. (The following is a generalisation describing what I guarantee is a common perception.) Builders and decorators tell you they'll call and don't, tell you they'll be with you tomorrow and don't turn up, tell you it'll take two weeks and end up taking four – yet they survive because people are crying out for their services. When the property market is booming estate agents don't need to be able to hard sell property – they can rely on customers buying. They send out salespeople who know nothing about the property they are trying to sell and they give no service to buyers because they know another will be along very soon.

The rewards and punishments in marketing

Rewards for satisfying customers	Punishment for failing to satisfy customers
They come back to you	They leave and don't come back
They tell others to go to you	They don't tell you why they are leaving
Reduced costs of doing business	They tell others never to go to you
Relationship allows you to understand needs even better	Continually acquiring new customers is costly

So in light of this, some people might say: 'Why bother being marketing oriented if I can make money without it?' Anyone can make money when times are good, but can you do so when times are bad – when buyers are not clamouring for houses or when there is not enough building work to go around for everyone? The real sign of a great business is one that is successful when times are not so easy – and that is when you really need to be marketing oriented – to guarantee you are satisfying customers better than your competitors can. In satisfying customers you get great rewards, and in failing to satisfy customers your business may be punished.

Even when times are great and you feel as though you don't have to try too hard (maybe, for example, there are no competitors offering anything that can compare to you), I urge any business to follow the marketing concept. Do not assume simply because the customer has no choice of supplier, or because you've got lots of work lined up and don't need to rely on this customer again for business, that this is sustainable in the long term. Two big reasons why:

1. A new competitor may enter your market at any time in the future, and having monitored your bare minimum efforts at customer satisfaction or your weaknesses as a business, they will be ripe to poach your customers.
2. Word will spread of your inability to satisfy or intent to satisfy customers, and with such a bad press it gets harder and harder to get customers, even when times are good, and almost impossible when times are bad.

You will need to keep looking for new customers, which in addition to being costly will eventually result in you running out of them.

Not to mention what the stupid customers do – tell all their mates never to buy from you – that is if Anne Robinson and *Watchdog* and all the other consumer affairs programmes haven't informed them first! It is a proven fact that it is cheaper for business to keep hold of its current customers than it is to keep looking for new ones. Of course there's nothing wrong with aiming to get new customers – it's part of the growth of your business. But if you find yourself being forced to find new customers because your old ones keep defecting to a competitor, eventually you're going to run out of customers to annoy! Keep your current customers *and* look to attract new ones.

HOW TO 'DO' MARKETING?

So how do you satisfy customers better than competitors can, and profitably? The key considerations in the marketing environment are given below.

This process of marketing is not going on in isolation, but in a dynamic and changing environment where tastes change, competitors come and go, opportunities and threats loom constantly. In the light of this being marketing oriented means:

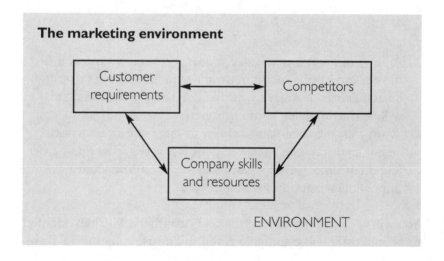

{10}

- identifying and anticipating exactly what the customer requirements are
- clarifying the skills, resources and ability of your company
- knowing what your competitors are doing/have the skills to do compared to you
- and then, deciding where to focus: which target customers and which requirements you can satisfy better than competitors can using skills you have got or can get.

Customer requirements

The only way to satisfy customers' requirements is to know what those requirements are, how they might change in the future and to understand their expectations – you can only satisfy people if you at least live up to, but, primarily, if you exceed expectations. Customer requirements are different and changing. You need to decide which need you intend to satisfy. Chapter 2 looks at this element of the marketing concept in more detail. Suffice it to say you really need to understand your customers – you need to have insight into the drivers of their needs and wants, some of which will be hidden, subconscious or embarrassing ones to which they don't want to admit.

Company skills and resources

Once you know what these requirements and expectations are, *stop*. Be realistic. Does your company really, honestly, absolutely have the skills needed to satisfy these customers? Make sure you know exactly what skills, resources and so on are needed, and honestly and objectively decide whether you have them or not. Cover everything: distribution coverage, staff skills, finances, accessibility, knowledge, staff numbers, staff attitude, customer service skills, technology, cost base and so on. (Depending on the market and business you are in or are going into, the list will be different.) If you discover that you are lacking the skills and ability, you have some choices to make – and making choices is one of the true signs of a company good at marketing:

Choice number 1 – Get the right skills and abilities (buy them or learn them), but do not try to compete without them.

Choice number 2 – Do not even try to satisfy the customers: you will fail, they'll be unhappy and never buy from you again, and maybe tell all their acquaintances never to think of using you. Instead, find customers whose requirements you can satisfy – be certain that customers have requirements that you can satisfy.

When Seagram Wine and Spirit company launched Absolut vodka in the UK in the early 1990s the target customers were to be found drinking in trendy city centre bars and clubs – *the* places to be seen. It was important to get Absolut stocked in these outlets. At that time the Seagram portfolio mainly comprised brands with older drinker profiles, which were stocked in more traditional pubs and clubs up and down the country – Captain Morgan rum, White Satin gin, Martell cognac. What Seagram lacked was a salesforce with a profile to match the outlets they were trying to get Absolut into, and a salesforce who understood the ways new bars operated in selling to younger drinkers. They knew that to try to launch Absolut without the proper sales representatives would have been folly, therefore they developed a small and dedicated resource whose aim was to focus on getting new outlets to stock the brand. As in choice 1 above, Seagram did not try to compete without the right skills or resources.

Being good at marketing means being clear about where to say no – one of the most difficult things to do when you are getting up and running and looking for business. Just be careful – don't get a reputation for failure early in the life of your business.

Competitors

Simply knowing customer requirements and expectations won't guarantee you satisfying them. Nor should you compete where you don't have the right skills. Why? Because as already mentioned, there's a group of not insignificant people out there calling themselves competitors who are also trying to satisfy customers – usually the same customers. If they can do the job better than you, then customers will buy from them (common sense if you are a customer). If these competitors have better skills and abilities, it will be they who profit.

Leger Holidays, founded in the early 1980s took coach parties to the Continent, but were finding themselves squeezed by competition from cheap flights and holidays. In 1993 they combated the threat by redirecting the company toward the short-break market, which was growing rapidly. They added a variety of themed short breaks to their repertoire, including visits to the Dutch bulb fields in spring, Second World War battle sites in Normandy and Monet's gardens at Giverny. They took 100 000 people to Disneyland Paris in 1999 alone. The strategy boosted profits 67 per cent a year between 1995 and 1998. They saw a growing area of the market, knew they could not compete where they were with huge competitors, so refocused on doing something different with the skills they had. If they had stayed where they were, they would have failed to profitably satisfy customers better than the competition.

WHAT MARKETING IS NOT

Marketing is not about conning people

You know – a misleading advert here and there, salesmen using hard pressure tactics, brochures promising one thing yet the business delivering another, promising great service only to have no one to answer queries or deal with problems. You can con someone, but only once. As we saw in the section on rewards for satisfying customers and punishments for failing to satisfy, you might be able to make people buy from you in the short term, but, if you fail to satisfy them, do you really think they and the friends they tell will be stupid enough to buy from you again?

Marketing is
not *about a 'hard' sell*

Of course marketing-focused companies need great salespeople or great sales techniques in order to get their offer to the customer and so satisfy them. But marketing is not about hard selling, not about finding as many new customers as possible irrespective of the real needs these customers have, not about getting new orders at any cost, not about ignoring service levels to current customers at the expense of new business, not about selling anything to anybody – the proverbial 'snow to an Eskimo' – rather it is about the efforts made to meet customer needs. When times get hard and companies wonder why their sales are down they immediately think it's the fault of the salespeople – instead they should be asking whether there is a need for their product or service at all any more.

Encyclopaedia Britannica sales had been falling for several years and the publisher could (perhaps initially they did?) have responded with a strong sales drive including incentives to their salespeople on every sale, price cuts and offers to potential customers. Long term this would have been to no avail. Why? The need that the *Encyclopaedia* is satisfying has a strong competitor now – computers and the Internet. People perceive that the encyclopaedias are no longer great value – they may look good on a shelf, but are expensive and quickly out of date compared to the information resource to be found on computer. *Encyclopaedia Britannica* had to change with the times and is now published on CD-Rom in order for it to stay competitive.

Marketing *is* not
assuming that cheapest is best

Producing a car only in black because that's a way to keep manufacturing costs down is fine as a strategy when there is no choice in the market. As soon as customers have a choice from a competitor there may be some who are willing to pay more for a car in blue.

Marketing is not *assuming that customers will want what you've got*

You may really believe that you have the best product or service in the world, but if customers don't perceive that then you are going to be in for a long and expensive battle to convince them otherwise. Marketing is about finding out what people want and making sure you can deliver it, as opposed to making something you think is great and hoping some customers will believe you. The British inventor Sir Clive Sinclair has learned to his cost the danger of going down this internally focused route – the Sinclair C5 environmentally friendly 'car' may technically have been brilliant, but the market was neither ready for it, nor perhaps were there enough people prepared to be seen looking ridiculous in public to cover the costs of its production. The Millennium Dome is another example – look how expensive it proved to be to convince customers to visit it. Although a bad press may have contributed to its poor performance, you must argue that if it had satisfied lots of visitors there would not have been so much bad press. The Dome management knew that whilst the largest tourist attraction in the UK currently drew 6 million visitors per year, they insisted on aiming for 12 million – a very internally focused objective.

Marketing is not *about doing things your way and your way only*

This approach is particularly common in the service industry. Dentists who never tell you up-front how much dental work will cost, interior designers who want to carry out work to their taste rather than to those of the customers, lawyers who never explain procedure but simply set the clock going as soon as the client enters his or her office. Thankfully competition is forcing the removal of many of these practices, but beware of becoming too focused on your own preferences and not paying enough attention to what would be best, easiest and most useful for the customer.

These five approaches may be successful for you – but probably only in the short term and not sustainable in the long term. If you put your needs as a business before the needs of the customer, you will fail to survive. Yes, you need to make money, but you cannot do this without focus on the customer and market. What a marketing focus will give you that other approaches do not is something called competitive advantage.

COMPETITIVE ADVANTAGE
– WHAT IT IS AND HOW TO GET IT

Have a think, from the customer's point of view, why it is that you might be better than your competitors. In the broadest sense it's likely to be because either:

- the customer can get from you the same as they can get elsewhere, but at a cheaper price or
- they can only get a certain something from you, something really important to them (it could be something tangible and real, or something perceived such as image).

If you offer either of the above, it is known as having competitive advantage.

As a business you may decide from the outset to follow either of these routes. If you are going down the first route, one thing is clear – you are going to have to have low costs compared to those of your competitors if you are going to stay profitable. This route to competitive advantage is therefore known as *cost leadership*. The alternative route is known as a *differentiation* approach – being different in the customer's eyes.

It is very hard to do both concurrently. In fact, many business leaders would say it is impossible, because in going for differentiation you usually need to incur costs which rule out cost leadership.

Cost leadership

The danger of a cost leadership approach for your small business is that large companies you may be competing against have huge economies of scale which make them automatically cheaper in many areas. In some areas your costs will be lower, especially in a service business (overheads such as wages, rent, administration, etc.). But what about manufacturing and raw material costs? Imagine trying to compete against Tesco in grocery prices, against Ikea for furniture prices or against Thomas Cook for holiday prices. So be realistic. Cost control in your business is of course essential, but beware of cutting costs in areas that affect the quality of your offer and thus affect your ability to satisfy customers. An example of this was a sex shop that was fined recently for selling videos that were not pornographic enough. The owner had been trying to cut costs and so bought in cheaper videos which, although pretty risqué, were not hard-core enough. Unsatisfied customers complained to Trading Standards officials. Cutting costs in essential areas may not get you fined, but it could result in unsatisfied and lost customers.

Differentiation

Many small businesses therefore need to consider the *differentiation* route to competitive advantage. The reward for being differentiated is that the customer may be prepared to pay a little more for the extra something they can't get elsewhere. This differentiation can come from anywhere. It might be tangible and physical, or an intangible perception or service element, or perhaps from the fun and enjoyable experience of dealing with you – as long as it is important to the customer. I know people who shop at one garden centre over another because its staff recommend planting suggestions at different times of year, they recommend colour and plant/soil suitability and have a help desk where an expert is available all day to answer queries on plant and garden problems.

It is becoming more and more difficult to differentiate, which is why the service and experience elements of what you do are so important – we will cover this in detail in Chapters 4 and 8.

There is a famous (or should that be infamous) Chinese restaurant in London's Chinatown. It is the only place I know of which manages to differentiate on the basis of the rudest service in a restaurant ('What do you mean how long will it be? You want fast food you go McDonald's!') – a risky strategy to follow!

As a contrast to that, there are three 'corner' shops on my street within 50 yards of my front door. How do they all survive? Differentiation – each doing something a little bit different. One has a small Post Office inside (yes, OK, it does have the usual accompanying queues) one bakes fresh bread daily and has an ATM (cash machine) while the other has the loveliest staff and sells stamps singly if you wish over the counter.

The problem with being a cost leader is that someone else will always try to lower his or her costs more. The problem with differentiation is that unless they're blind, competitors will probably try to muscle in on your little scheme that is winning friends and success. Staying ahead of the game means maintaining your competitive advantage or, in business jargon, achieving sustainable competitive advantage.

HOW TO MAINTAIN COMPETITIVE ADVANTAGE

To follow the general path to sustainable competitive advantage you need to:

- keep closest to changing customer requirements
- get insight into customers to monitor trends and changing habits
- ensure your skills are up to date and not getting a bit 'rusty'
- anticipate competitors copying you
- remain flexible
- keep searching for innovative ways to be *the* differentiated offer in the market (Chapter 4 and onwards look at this in detail).

Specifically, maintaining competitive advantage involves always speaking to your customers. Keep asking them what it is that they really value about your offer. Find out why they remain satisfied. Are you the easiest to order from, have you the friendliest staff and provide the most helpful advice, the speediest repair service, the widest range and guaranteed in stock? Are you the quickest to respond, do you always keep people up to date with developments? And keep doing these things. More importantly, and this will sound a bit like opening the floodgates, you should make it as easy as possible for your customers to complain. Indeed, encourage them to complain. An honest and confident company will have no problems with this. Look at it as free market research: people giving you the chance to put things right and improve. Chapter 8 will look further at the logic behind doing this, but suffice it to say for now that most customers don't complain; they simply walk away and never buy from that source again. It is better to have the chance to put things right. But, and more on this again later, *never* ask people for feedback on what you are doing wrong and should improve on and then ignore what they say. It is better not to ask at all than to ask and not do anything with the suggestions. I think of my years living in hotels up and down the country where I took the time (yes, I took the time, my own time!) to complete those questionnaires they put in your bedroom. 'Help us improve our service.' 'How can we make things better for you?' they say. Every month for the next eight months the same questionnaires are there, and apparently they have done nothing with my suggestions.

Another way to have competitive advantage, especially differentiation, is to take advantage of something that large companies really envy you for: the flexibility that comes with your small size. Responding quickly to changes in the market, being flexible enough to change your skills as well as your processes when the market demands it. This is, I think, just one of the areas, albeit a very important one, where small businesses have an advantage over large. The large organisation has company policies in place, complicated systems and procedures driving and monitoring actions, and layers of management through which changes must be authorised and permission gained. Ask anyone in big business about things they dislike and they may, among many things, mention how slow it is to get things to market, to implement changes, to fight company politics and how they seem to be reactive rather than proactive. Use this to your advantage, and remember it as your business grows – do not let size impede your flexibility or willingness to adapt and stay ahead and get things done. You are in a great position to act and change quickly.

C&A, the clothing retailer, have withdrawn from the UK high street. They had no competitive advantage and the family business could no longer afford to carry on. They were neither a cost leader nor had they any differentiation to offer customers. Their cost base was too high compared to the competition and therefore they could no longer afford to compete on price. Meanwhile their clothing range was no longer pleasing customers compared to what was on offer elsewhere for a similar price, therefore they couldn't compete on differentiation either – they were stuck in the middle.

Most small businesses start because they have identified a gap in the market. It is a fact that businesses that do best are those that have spotted a *real* gap – of course that alone is not enough, as you then have to go on to provide a perfect offering to fill that gap. But that's what later chapters will cover. Let's concentrate now on the gap where there is really a need for what you can offer.

IS THERE REALLY A NEED FOR YOUR OFFER?

A gap exists when the market is full of customers crying out for a product or service and not enough suppliers to provide it. A gap also exists when there is an opportunity to do something better than or differently to those already in the market, or to provide a benefit to customers: a solution that no one has thought of.

Think of it this way – what do customers buy from you if you are a window cleaner? Clean windows, a friendly chat, reliability that you'll turn up every six weeks. What about the corner shop? Life-saving essential ingredients for tonight's meal and a saved journey to the supermarket. The definition of the solution that fills the gap is: the thing you will do that adds value to the potential customers – *the opportunity to offer them benefits*. A gap is not just something that you think exists, you've got to be sure people out there are going to want what you have to offer and perceive that it gives them benefits they can't get elsewhere.

Andy Pollock used to work for Ernst & Young accountancy firm when he spotted a gap in the market – for a small accountancy firm that could really understand the difficulties facing small- and medium-sized companies. He always thought that small businesses were not well looked after by his profession and saw there were comparable service providers for them, doing well, in the legal area. He saw a law firm set up in 1983 with 20 people, giving the same quality advice as the major firms, but with the attention of a small one. Rees Pollock was born.

Cannon Avent, a company founded to make rubber accessories, are one of the UK's fastest growing private companies. The MD Edward Atkin, after the birth of his son, realised how 'totally useless' most baby-feeding products were. The tall baby bottle common all over the world was impractical and unstable for pouring in formula. He knew there was a very real opportunity (he'd heard his wife complain about them enough I'm sure) to do things differently and better. After some time Atkin had a redesigned bottle: a short stubby container made of polycarbonate, with a wide teat to make it as much like a breast as possible. Now Cannon Avent make a variety of baby-feeding products, including bottles, breast pumps and pacifiers, and have driven up their share of the British baby-feeding market from 4 per cent to 40 per cent. Atkin attributes their impressive results to making a few products, each one genuinely better than anything else in the market.

Be realistic too, remember what we said about competitive advantage – you may think that Tesco and the other supermarkets have left a gap in the market through the way they treat their customers, but taking them on at grocery retailing for the family weekly shop is unrealistic. You will never be able to compete on price with the giants – they have such bargaining power over suppliers that they can buy at much lower prices than you could ever compete with. Instead, why not see if in your local area there is demand for a local shop supplying niche products with great service.

You may think that MFI and Ikea have left a gap for you to do better in furniture, but again be realistic. You would never be able to compete with the mass manufacture of furniture on that scale – do something they can't or won't do, such as making things to individual specification – if you know that there is a demand for that out there.

Artizian Catering Services were founded in 1997 and are already turning over almost £3.3 million. Rather than typical 'canteens'

Artizian run workplace restaurants where the food is fresh and modern, the menu varied and the surroundings colourful and exciting. The huge advertising agency Ogilvy & Mather recently gave Artizian an £800 000 contract after a director saw what they had to offer when visiting a client's premises where Artizian were supplying the lunchtime fare. Their mission is clear: 'To make eating in the office canteen an exciting experience.' They realise that eating is an emotive experience and should be fun, making customers feel they are getting out of the office at lunchtime.

So, that's marketing. It is not just about reaching customers and making them want what you have to offer. It is knowing what benefits they are looking for, what competitors are not providing, having the skills and ability to offer solutions profitably. It is satisfying them so well that you occupy their mind as *the* provider (called having a high share of mind of the customer) and then ensuring you keep that share and the relationship that comes with it.

SUMMARY CHECKLIST

- Put customers first in everything you do
- Do something better than or different from anyone else
- Make sure it stays better or different
- Make sure the gap really exists – make sure people do see the need for something better or different (or you'll have a hard time and need a big budget convincing them)
- Recognise whether you have the skills to compete: if not then don't, or get the skills
- Anticipate changing customer requirements – so remain insightful
- Monitor changing conditions – trends, competitors, etc.
- Keep your skills up to date in line with changing market requirements
- Once you have won the customers make sure you keep them.

2
Who Is the Customer?
(and what do they really want)

In the factory we make cosmetics; in the store we sell hope.
Charles Revlon

THE CHAPTER AT A GLANCE

Marks & Spencer, BHS, Rover – all huge companies with reputations and money to spend on getting their business in order. All are having a hard time trying to satisfy customers better than competitors and make a profit. Customers are dissatisfied and loyalty declines along with profits. If they can't get it right with all their years of experience, it can have a pretty daunting effect on many a small business endeavouring to succeed in a difficult environment. Yet many small businesses have been performing so much better than these giants.

The fundamental problem with these troubled companies seems to be that they don't know who the customer is that they are trying to appeal to and what it is that those customers really want. If you don't know who your typical customer is, how do you know what style of clothing to sell, what prices to set, what style of store to have, what image to portray? If you don't know who your target customer is, how do you know what design of car to manufacture, what options to offer and where and how to advertise?

If you are not clear about the people and their associated needs that your business is attempting to address, you run the danger of being stuck in the middle, pleasing no one fully. Customers will reluctantly make do until someone else comes along, someone who understands them and their real needs much better – someone who can satisfy those needs.

This chapter is designed to make it clear why you need to define and target specific customers, give examples of how to go about this, and share the rewards of getting it right.

THE DIFFERING NEEDS OF PEOPLE

It is your responsibility as a business to understand customers well enough to identify what it is that they *really* want. This is why customer understanding and targeting is one of the main features of the marketing iceberg – a key part of beneath the surface that supports the tactics.

Understanding the basics of human behaviour tells us that people have different levels of needs and wants. Some people are more than happy just to wear a plain white M&S T-shirt while others will only be satisfied with one that comes from Armani or Burberry. Some needs are basic and obvious whilst others are more complex and hidden. Refusing to accept the need for any customers to buy expensive brands and labels is refusing to accept human nature. Understanding customers is therefore a complex and challenging task in running your business – but one that will set you

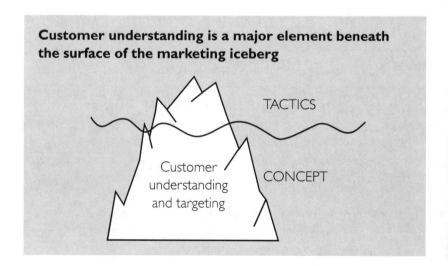

Customer understanding is a major element beneath the surface of the marketing iceberg

TACTICS

Customer understanding and targeting

CONCEPT

far ahead of the game. Too many people assume everyone out there has the same needs and tastes as they do.

So you must try to find out the needs that exist in your market among customers, current or potential. (Chapter 3 looks at how to find customer information.) This will require you to be very insightful – considering not just the rational, but also the emotional needs you are really satisfying. Identify which needs your competitors are satisfying more or less well, and which needs are not well catered for – this could be an opportunity to stand out from the crowd.

Consider this example. Pantene shampoo obviously satisfies the need for clean hair. However, it is satisfying much more than that. Clean hair is shiny hair, and shiny hair is more beautiful – people want to have beautiful looking hair, that's the real need. Other competitors in the market were saying: 'Our shampoo gives you strong healthy hair.' But some customers, especially young women, thought: 'Tough, I want beautiful hair, who cares if it's healthy!' A subtle difference maybe, but enough to make one brand successful and its competitor not. The problem is that every individual probably wants something slightly (or hugely) different from everyone else. Even with a book such as this – you probably want something different from another reader.

What I need from a clothing store may be completely different on some levels to that of my friends, mother and colleagues. What I need from a car may be totally different from those of my brother or husband or friends. What do you want from a good night out? What does your partner want? What about your parents or children?

Take a huge global industry for a second – the car industry, one that has seen varying degrees of success at profit and customer satisfaction. What do people need from a car? Consider just four needs in that market:

Need 1   some people simply want to get from A to B
Need 2   some are interested in safety and reliability
Need 3   some value fuel efficiency and low service costs making the car as economical to run as possible
Need 4   some need the car to demonstrate their success and status.

And of course the needs could go on: the need to look trendy and turn heads, the need for speed, the need for independence. So as a car manufacturer what do you do? At one extreme you could produce one car that you hope will please everyone or at the other produce something different for every single individual.

Can you imagine one car satisfying every potential customer, each of whom wants something different? You may please one or two people, but probably please no one fully. The people who want speed go for the car designed specifically for that purpose. Those who want just to get from A to B choose the car designed with this in mind, those who need to prove their success and status go for the car that can do that perfectly. And what happens to you who have tried to please everyone? You get stuck in the middle, not really pleasing anyone. And how do you have to compete? Usually on price. Constant store sales and special offers are occasionally a sign of not understanding the real customer or need.

As for producing something different for every individual, how easy or practical is it to really please each and every individual in the market with a specially tailored and produced offer – and, remember, at the same time make money? As an author I could never write a different book for each and every potential reader.

This is a very real challenge for your business. Which customers and needs are you going to try to satisfy? Are you trying to please too many customers all with different needs and in the end pleasing no one? Are you losing money in trying to please every single customer? Are you giving out contradictory messages to customers? Will teenagers come to the hairdressing salon that their grand-mother goes to? Will my uncle the wine-buff believe he can get his weekly treat and expert advice in the same store his sister buys her Leibfraumilch? Will my materialistic and *nouveau riche* boss enjoy taking his even more materialistic wife to a fancy restaurant for dinner when that restaurant starts to draw in kids' parties offering pizza and cake?

What you must do as a business is make choices about which customers and needs you wish to satisfy and focus on them – if you try to satisfy everyone you'll satisfy no one totally. So how can you go about choosing which customers to target?

The differing needs from a car

Segment	Customers	Need
1	Price-conscious value seekers	To get from A → B
2	Mr and Mrs Dependable	Safety and reliability
3	Mr and Mrs Efficient	Fuel efficiency and low service costs
4	Mr 'I have arrived'	To demonstrate their success and status

AN APPROACH TO SATISFYING CUSTOMERS

The ideal would of course be to treat everyone as an individual and so satisfy their needs. Assuming this is impossible (unless you are in the sort of industry which only has a few big customers) what you can do is group together people who have broadly similar needs. Marketing people would call it segmentation.

Using the car example in the table above, you may as a business decide that there are four broad segments of needs and customers. As you can imagine, an actual car for each segment would look totally different. As a car company, you must choose which of these four segments you will target. Which of these segments are you going to satisfy better than competitors can – 1, 2, 3, 4 or all? Whichever you pick are called your target markets.

Think about a real example: Ford Motors. Do they produce one car and hope it appeals to everyone? Of course not. They have carefully identified segments and produced models for those they wish to target. Think about how you would describe the customers whom the following Ford cars are aimed at. Try to describe the target market in as much detail as possible rather than simply saying man or woman, over 30 or under 50:

- the Jaguar XK8
- the Puma
- the classic Jaguar
- the Cougar
- the Fiesta
- the Focus.

Think about other car companies – such as Mercedes. Now Mercedes as a whole are targeting a specific segment – probably those with a bit of money to spend! But they split this market further down into segments at which the following models are targeted:

- the A-class   - the SLK
- the estate   - the E-class.

Think how you would describe, in detail, the customers of the following:

- Disneyland Paris   - Thomas Pink shirtmakers
- Nike   - Marks & Spencer
- Next   - Aldi
- Sainsbury's   - Harrods
- Harvey Nicholls.

Maybe you couldn't manage to be specific or insightful about the target. That's fine. Maybe you don't know enough about the companies to be able to answer. Or maybe it says something about the company itself – do they know whom they are really targeting?

WHY YOU NEED TO SEGMENT

Hopefully the answer is obvious.

Segmentation is such an important part of what you need to do – if I were asked to give only one piece of advice to small businesses, it would be the need to be absolutely crystal clear about which customers and needs are you aiming to satisfy. Everything that you are thinking of doing comes from this description of your target customer – what you will offer, where you'll offer it, the price you'll charge and so on. If you can't describe the customer, how on earth can you make decisions about what to look like, say, sound or sell? Unless you are a clear cost leader in the market, you can't afford to get 'stuck in the middle' competing on price. It is a downward spiral to lost profit. By segmenting you can see where best to concentrate your efforts and money and skills in a way that you can clearly have competitive advantage.

So, close your eyes and picture clearly in your mind how your customer will look as they walk through the door into your shop, office or wherever you'd come into contact with them. The picture should be as clear as possible. Can you describe what they wear, how old they are, where they live, who their friends would be, where they shop and drink, what they do for a living and in their spare time? OK, maybe not that clearly yet, but by the time you start pulling your offer together you should, in fact must, be able to! You must think more about the segments. Get people around to help you and to add to your thinking. That's what we'll look at now.

HOW TO SEGMENT

You're opening a coffee shop. You need to decide which sort of customers and needs to target. First of all you must segment the market into the alternatives. Your segments might be based on the customers' ages, cultures, whether they have children or not and whether attitudinally they are coffee connoisseurs or simply relaxation seekers or quick-stop pick-me-uppers.

You are opening a restaurant. What are all the alternative segments you could target?

You are making bread. What are the alternative segments? People who are on a diet, people who are allergic to wheat, people who are

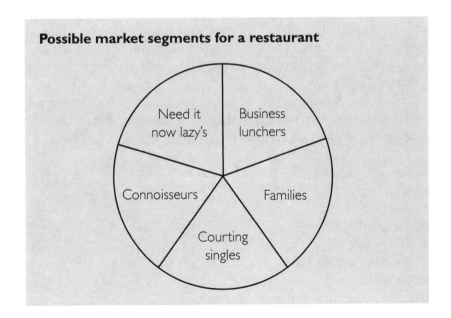

Possible market segments for a restaurant

- Need it now lazy's
- Business lunchers
- Connoisseurs
- Families
- Courting singles

organically inclined, mothers with kids who need tasty sandwich bread? The geography of where customers live or were brought up is also a key segmentation measure in the food industry. I was told once that bread manufacturers need to make sweeter bread for its Scottish customers than for its English ones. Two totally different segments – one type of bread would be too sweet for some and not sweet enough for others.

You are a training company providing training services to managers. What are the alternative segments? Small companies, junior managers, middle managers, senior managers, international companies, marketing-focused companies, IT companies, financial companies, growing companies? The trick with segmenting your market is to identify all the things that really make people have different needs. In this example, junior managers and senior managers quite clearly have different training needs and are two different segments – occupation, age and experience cause them to have different needs – while in the restaurant example families and courting couples clearly have different needs – attitude and family stage cause that to be the case.

Think about women's magazines: age causes people to have different needs (along, of course, with personality, attitude, presence of children, hobbies, being single or married, occupation and so on). Think about newspapers: occupation or political viewpoint may cause readers to have different needs. Can you imagine a newspaper not being clear about which customer it was targeting?

There are hundreds of reasons that make customers have different needs that make segmentation difficult, but it doesn't mean you shouldn't try. Consider:

- age
- sex
- where they live
- the job they do
- the money they earn
- the religion they have
- social class
- family stage they are in

- personality and attitude
- leisure, hobbies they enjoy
- specific benefits they are looking for.

Likewise if you are selling to other businesses, consider:

- how big they are
- how many employees they have
- the industry they are in
- their attitude to risk
- how they are owned
- geography they are in
- specific benefits they are looking for.

Now let's look at some examples of how some companies have actually segmented. Coca-Cola may decide that there are customer segments with the following characteristics, each looking for something slightly different from a soft drink:

care-nots	health is not an issue, just give me a refreshing drink
weight worriers	don't make my drink fattening
sleep deprived's	please don't contribute to keeping me awake
hypochondriac	everything is so bad for you, make it healthy.

As a result Coca-Cola have decided to target all four segments and have produced, respectively, regular Coke, Diet Coke, Caffeine free Coke and Caffeine free Diet Coke. In some markets there aren't that many 'hypochondriacs' so they don't bother trying to sell the Caffeine free Diet Coke there at all.

The weather is an issue if you have a car. Oil companies therefore use geography as a way to segment. The engine oil for a car at the Equator needs to be different to that in northern climes.

An American company called Quidel operates in the pregnancy test kit market. They could have said that the segments are decided by age, or family stage, or religion. But they realised that the key for a woman was whether she wanted to be pregnant or not – thus their segments are the hopefuls and the fearfuls.

The more you understand your customers the easier segmentation is – the more insightful you are the more likely you are to know the differing needs people really have. Once you have segmented the market, it is up to you to decide which of the segments you will target. Before you can decide the menu, the atmosphere, the music you play, the staff you employ, the location you open in, the prices you can charge in your coffee shop, you need to decide if you are targeting the coffee connoisseur or the trendy teenager and 20 somethings or the mothers with kids.

DECIDING WHERE TO TARGET AND FOCUS

You are an accountant who has identified four segments: the high-wealth individuals needing tax-avoiding savings advice; the medium-sized growing companies needing tax, legal and investment appraisal advice and support; the small sole-trader needing her annual tax return completed; and the risk-taking entrepreneur needing fast and innovative business advice.

Do you decide to target all of them? One only, and if so which one? Perhaps two or three of them. In order to decide you need to consider the following:

- Do you have the skills and resources to successfully satisfy the segment(s)?
- Specifically, what financial resources do you have?
- What segments are your competitors successfully targeting?
- What are your strengths and weaknesses compared to your competitors?
- Is the segment likely to grow in the future?
- How big is the segment and how profitable?
- How easy is it to reach this segment and communicate with them?

In the Quidel pregnancy kit example they decided to target both the hopefuls and fearfuls and therefore had to produce two different offers. They could equally have decided to target only one of the segments. However, they saw both segments as attractive in terms of growth and profitability, considered that the competitors had not understood the needs of the customers well enough to target them, and they had the resources to develop a specific pregnancy kit for both. While targeting only one segment gives you complete focus and brings you even closer to the needs of the customers in that segment, there is the danger of putting all your eggs in one basket. If the segment is very unstable and likely to be based on trends or fads, it may be dangerous to focus so heavily on one.

However, there are difficulties that come with trying to target more than one segment which can't be ignored. I heard a story relating to a hotel in Spain and the problems it had in trying to go for two different segments where really its skills and resources didn't enable it to do so.

The hotel had decided that because of seasonality it would target in the wintertime the OAPs from Britain who would spend months on end in the resort as it was cheaper than paying heating bills back home. In summertime it targeted the teenagers and 20-somethings who descended for non-stop hedonism, raves and cultural revelry. Fine, two distinct segments each with very different needs.

But with two distinct problems as well.

First, can you imagine how different the facilities required for both segments are? Everything from the décor, the staff, the food, the alcohol, the entertainment, the busy times of day?

Second, and probably more of a disaster for the hotel, imagine that difficult time of year: the late spring and early summer season, when there is likely to be a mixture of both segments in the hotel. A recipe for disaster I think. Loud music, loud guests, non-stop parties, room swapping – and then you have to consider what the 20-somethings and teenagers might get up to. Perhaps it should have concentrated on the older clientele all year round, and not approached Club 18–30 to feature the hotel in its brochure.

Make sure the segment on which you will focus your efforts is big enough now, or in the future, to warrant all the work you'll put in. Imagine you sell candles, all sorts of candles. Now you may have identified, as I did recently, that some people could put candles to quite an unusual use. There is a segment of the market (mainly teenage boys who wear trousers with the bums down to the backs of their knees and spend free time rollerblading and skateboarding) that has a need for candles. Would you believe that they rub the candles onto walls, steps and benches to make the surfaces friction free and as slippery as possible – it looks quite impressive to mount the obstacles and slide precariously along each. Now according to the rules of segmentation, they are a distinct group with specific needs. But I'm not sure as a candle seller that the segment is (a) large enough to focus on solely or (b) profitable enough to justify concentrating all your efforts on, perhaps not even some of your efforts. On top of this you are probably running the risk of being criticised for encouraging kids to 'vandalise' public property for leisure purposes. Taking a marketing approach and identifying the opportunities in the market first, somebody somewhere might equate such trends as rubbing candles on walls, as an opportunity to provide tailored goods and services for boarders and bladers. Just be sure that any kids who currently use cheap candles for waxing purposes would be prepared to trade up to 'boarders' wax'.

THE DANGERS OF NOT BEING CLEAR

The punishment for not really having or going for a clear target group of customers can easily be shown. Forgive me for using the examples mentioned early in the introduction to the chapter – but they represent the dangers so well.

In April 2000 Philip Green bought all 155 BHS stores from the Storehouse group in an attempt to turn them around. Even though it had the potential to pick up business as its main competitor M&S was having severe problems, the troubled retail business had sales and profits declining year on year. Even before getting underneath the BHS business to understand the problems in detail Philip said that the main trouble with the brand was that 'it is not really clear who their customer is anymore'. They got caught in the rut of constantly having to have 'sales' to sell off stock.

Growth in the market was coming from value retailers like Matalan, Peacocks and Primark, which claim to offer clothing of similar quality, but at much lower prices, and at the other end from specialist retailers like Kookai, Jigsaw and Next – which could offer consumers good quality, more stylish clothing and from whom consumers see the opportunity to get something a little bit different. Continually selling at cheap prices is cluttered and bargain basement – and very dangerous if it makes you compete against value retailers who do not have the high costs of your prime store location and space to deal with.

On 15 June 2000 C&A announced that they were closing all of their UK outlets. They were finding it impossible to remain profitable. Their sales were declining and their stores were located in prime locations where the costs of property and rates were immense. They weren't fashionable enough for the younger market or cheap enough for the price-driven segment. They had totally lost sight of who their target customer was. Their only saving grace has been that rather than renting, they owned their stores and could amass millions by selling the prime property to the likes of Next and Gap.

That great British institution, M&S has had precisely the same worries recently. Profits have been falling, quality concerns have been rising, the icon of everything held up as successful Britain was for the first time being publicly criticised. Their clothing collections have received mixed reactions. It seemed that they couldn't please anyone. The fashion conscious found the stores and merchandise bland and dull. The traditional middle-class and middle-aged female shopper said the styles were too young and there was nothing for them. The Buy-British loyalists complained as they found more and more stock being sourced and manufactured abroad as the strength of the pound made it cheaper to import goods. In an attempt to improve their image they launched a new range of clothing called Autograph. Premium quality, slightly more avant-garde designs under the Autograph brand, designed by great British designers such as Betty Jackson, Matthew Williamson and Julian MacDonald. They have also been working with Agent Provocateur (doyenne of the crotch-less knicker) to offer a range of extremely sexy underwear. Industry pundits claim that the root of their problems has been, again, total confusion around who their customer is.

I am sure these companies did all consider carefully the segmentation of the customer and select target markets on which they intended to focus – but probably some time ago. People change, needs change – segments come and go – it is just as dangerous to segment once and forget about it forever as it is to never segment at all.

REWARDS FOR GETTING SEGMENTATION RIGHT

There are four main rewards for getting your segmentation right:

- ▪ strategy setting is easier
- ▪ you are closer to your customers
- ▪ it is easier to make choices
- ▪ differentiation is more likely.

Strategy setting is easier

Having a clear target market makes your strategy for satisfying them so much easier. It helps you clarify the benefits you must offer and how to offer them. It makes decisions on your coffee shop decoration, menu, pricing, staff, and location all so much simpler. It helps you focus on why you are going to be better than other coffee shops at satisfying and therefore keeping hold of your target customers.

The owner of a fabulous local taxi firm was telling me how well business was going recently. He thought it was down to knowing what different customers wanted. He said he targeted three main types of customer:

1. Business people – People in the town who travel a lot on business – to meetings, to offices, to airports, to clients they need to impress. He makes sure the driver looks smart, the car

is clean and upmarket, the car is always on time and that the account at the end of the month is accurate.

2. Wealthy ladies – These ladies don't drive and would never dream of taking public transport. They go shopping in Harrods once a week and need an expensive looking car to take them there and be flexible enough to wait around all day until they are ready to come home. Price is not an issue.

3. 'Party-over's' – Closing time at the pubs and people are desperate to get home. They don't care what the car looks like, usually don't mind if it doesn't turn up right on time and know they'll be paying a premium to insure against upholstery staining.

Fortunately he has different cars he uses for the third segment – without this resource he says he'd leave this target market alone. He couldn't afford to risk losing the two main target markets where he has complete competitive advantage and strong customer loyalty.

Closer to customers

In targeting specific customers your experiences in delivering your strategy allow you to understand them even better, which goes on to make it easier to satisfy them. A circle of customer understanding and satisfaction.

Easier to make choices

Sometimes in business, especially a small and growing business, there is a great temptation to say yes to every piece of work and to every customer. The danger is that you say yes before you realise you are not as skilled as you should be to really satisfy the customer, and as a result they won't give you a second chance. The whole process of understanding how the market is segmented and identifying the one(s) you will target is so helpful for choosing whom to say yes and no to.

Secondly, will the customer conflict with the core of your business success? Let me give you an example. Imagine you are making and selling a product that is getting a good name for itself and a loyal following. You sell it through city centre boutiques, fashionable outlets where customers are able to enjoy a sumptuous shopping experience and are happy to pay the premium price in return for the cachet, the style and the personal enjoyment. You still need to broaden your distribution base in order to cover many of your costs and are looking for new outlets through which to sell your product. Retailer X has approached you – they have 120 stores across the country – result! This distribution may solve your financial concerns in the short term. Go back to your plans and read the description of the target market for your product. See how it matches the type of customers buying in the stores of retailer X. If retailer X also has a reputation for being a bit pile it high and sell 'em cheap, imagine the effect on your other loyal retailers who see X slashing prices and therefore profit margins. Levi's image has suffered among the important trend-setting teenage jean wearers, those willing to pay a price for fashion. They abandoned the brand when they saw it for sale in places they didn't associate with high fashion and style. So segmentation might be the thing that helps you make choices.

Differentiation

As competition increases it gets harder and harder to sustain competitive advantage. One route may be through segmentation. If you can spot a need and a group of customers who are currently not being served well by the competition, you could develop a differentiated offer and establish loyalty before the competition even realise another segment exists.

Segmentation is always going to be a compromise – a compromise because it's not possible to create a different thing for every different reader, shopper, driver or business. It is up to you how far you segment. There is no right or wrong answer. The aim is for your business to identify a particular group of people with specific requirements that you are in a position to please, profitably.

SUMMARY CHECKLIST

- Customers have different needs
- Clarify precisely which customers and needs you are aiming to target and satisfy
- Focus on this segment once it is chosen
- Don't get stuck in the middle – or you'll end up competing on price
- Prioritise your segments if you are dealing with more than one
- Make sure you have the skills and resources to satisfy the segment – always
- Watch competitors to see how they approach segments
- Tailor your strategy to satisfy each segment.

3
Monitoring Your Business Environment
The why, the what and the how

Standing still is the fastest way to move
backwards in a rapidly changing world.
Anon

THE CHAPTER AT A GLANCE

Being a marketing-oriented business will help you stay ahead of the game. The ability to satisfy target customers better than your competitors, profitably, by using your skills and resources should not be taken for granted. What worked last year or even last month may not work next year or next month. The environment you are operating in is ever changing. Customers' tastes change, competitors' skills change, market conditions change. Skills and resources you had on which to base your success become irrelevant and out of date. You lose your competitive advantage and you fail to satisfy customers. The only way to avoid this is to constantly monitor the environment in which you are running your business – this is known as being externally focused. Being externally focused helps you develop strategies that are effective in your competitive market.

This chapter looks in more detail at why it is important to be externally focused and monitor your environment, but specifically it helps you identify which areas you need to monitor and how to go about gathering the information you may need. Don't be daunted by the amount of information you may need – you'll quickly be able to prioritise that which is most relevant to your business and your market.

WHY YOU NEED TO BE EXTERNALLY FOCUSED

If you are a new business you need to know:

■ Does the need for my products or services really exist?
■ How big is the market and what is its potential?
■ Which customers should I target?
■ What competitors are doing that I could do better?

If you have been in business for some time then quite simply you do not want to become:

■ uncompetitive
■ left behind
■ the one that missed out.

■ illegal
■ out of favour

You may have been the most favoured supplier in your market for some time – continually satisfying customers better than competitors, keeping customers coming back to you and building great relationships with them. The danger of being so good is one of complacency. Not noticing how much your competitors are improving their offer, not noticing how customer expectations have changed a little since you started in business – generally doing what you've always done because up until now it has always worked really well for you. Before long you've slipped from being the best in the market to second or third – not by doing anything different, but by standing still, ignoring changes going on around you externally.

This is why people talk about marketing as being externally focused. Marketing as a process is going on in a dynamic constantly changing business environment. Things are happening out there that you must monitor, consider or respond to. If you don't know these things are happening, or might happen, you risk taking the wrong road, you face huge threats to your business, or miss great opportunities to go on satisfying customers profitably.

Imagine a business such as that of a painter and decorator. Think of all the trends and changes in their business environment that have affected their business. Wallpapering is no longer the obvious route to decorating walls (so much so that even huge companies like ICI have pulled out of the manufacture of wallpaper paste), the demand for paint of every colour imaginable is massive, the ease of using paint on walls has minimised the need for a professional decorator in many households. Professionals have had to change to keep up and remain a valuable service. They need to be experts at paint effects that Joe public can't easily do themselves (sponging, rag rolling, scum ball glazing and so on). They need to realise that people may want to spend less on the job, but repeat it and update the decoration much more often – they need to stay externally focused. The painter and decorator who doesn't stay ahead of the game is one who ignores or fails to spot these changes in the business environment and carries on doing what he or she has always done, because it used to work.

Imagine you are the retailer of gents' shirts, dress shirts to wear with suits and ties: a Thomas Pink or a Charles Tyrwhitt perhaps. These retailers cannot afford to ignore the huge trend of the moment: the move to more casual dress at work. Even the big City companies such as Arthur Andersen, the bastions of traditional city dress, have embraced the move to a less formal dress policy. If you are Thomas Pink, you could choose to ignore the trend and remain steadfast in your focus on shirts to wear with suits and ties. Or you might see the trend as being so wide reaching, so permanent a move, that to ignore it would be short sighted. In fact Thomas Pink and most companies like them have developed a range of shirts specifically to be worn as the smart casual look in the dress-down office. They have become externally focused.

The same holds true for small companies selling carpets. If you are going to remain solely in the retailing and fitting of carpets, make sure the segment of customers you are targeting is large enough. In some parts of the country small carpet companies have found it too hard to compete against the trend for floorboards and rugs as an alternative floor covering. If floorboards are not your area of expertise, but you predict that this is where the market will move to, then make sure you acquire the appropriate skills. Alternatively you may decide that a certain segment will always want carpets and this is where you will focus. At least by remaining externally focused you have actively made the decision and are aware of the trends and changing habits that may affect you.

To continue the theme, I imagine that you'll have noticed the way TV of the moment seems to be one big series of house, room, gardening and personal improvement shows. Pity the small garden centre that fails to ignore the changing tastes of its customers. If your target market has embraced the need to returf, repaint, replant, pot and prune and redesign their gardens and you have not responded by offering products to allow this, you are automatically uncompetitive. I know you may never have stocked wood paint for fences or gazebos in lilac or terracotta, but if that's the demand of your target market you have to respond to it.

Staying competitive, keeping hold of customers, remaining profitable requires you therefore to consider many things. The next section looks at the general areas you should monitor – all of which are relevant to you, no matter the type of business you are operating or are starting.

WHAT YOU NEED TO CONSIDER AND MONITOR

In Chapter 1, I introduced a simple visual (see p. 10) to represent the marketing environment. At this stage let's investigate what makes up this environment in detail – these are the areas you need to consider and monitor. I have illustrated the three core elements of the marketing concept (customers, competitors and company skills) in a slightly different way here, but the meaning is still the same (see p. 44).

First, of course, your environment includes your customers. But not just your current customers. It includes your potential customers, too. Second, obviously, your environment includes your competitors. But again, not just your current competitors, but any potential new entrants into your market. Substitutes are an important consideration. Substitutes are a form of indirect competitor. By substitute we mean any other product or service that could satisfy the same need as your offer. Coca-Cola, for example, look at the competition in terms of other cola drinks, soft drinks, juices and waters, but they might also consider ice cream or crisps

The marketing environment in detail

as substitutes. When a 10-year-old has their pocket money they may decide to buy an ice cream instead of a can of Coke.

Your environment also comprises any distributors you use or could use or whom others use to get their offer to the end customer.

The other areas you must consider are those outside your immediate environment, and while you have no control over these, you must monitor them, anticipate them and consider their impact on your business. These areas are sometimes together called PESTLE simply because the acronym relates to the areas to be considered:

- **P**olitical trends
- **E**conomic trends
- **S**ocial trends
- **T**echnological trends
- **L**egal trends
- **E**nvironmental trends.

Let's look in more detail at precisely what you are monitoring in each of the above areas and shown in the diagram opposite.

Competitors

Who are they currently? What do they do particularly well? Is there anything they're not so good at? Do they have specific skills or capabilities you don't have? Where do you think they are most vulnerable? What do customers think about this competitor and their products or services? How do they produce, distribute and sell their offers? How is your offer different to theirs and why should your customers buy from you and not them? What prices do they charge? What discounts do they offer? How do your competitors communicate with customers? Who supplies your competitors? What about new entrants into the market? How easy is it for them to break in to the market? Are there any barriers to entry that you could build?

Customers

Is your target market profile changing? Is it as large a segment as it was? Are your products or services still satisfying their needs? Have their needs changed? How loyal are they? Why do they buy from you? What do they see as being critical that you get right? How do they perceive the value you offer? How is your image perceived? What do they think you are particularly strong or weak at? If you have a retail business do you understand the actual people who come in to shop? You may be targeting your clothes at teenage boys, but is it them that buys or is it their mothers?

Arcadia is the retail giant that owns stores such as Dorothy Perkins, Top Shop, Principles and Wallis. They have done lots of research which identified that at least 60 per cent of their men's clothing was bought by or under the influence of women – as a result they have closed branches of Principles for Men, combined Burtons Menswear with Dorothy Perkins and Top Man with Top Shop. A good example of the importance of customer and shopper understanding.

Suppliers

Who are they and where are they? How powerful are they? Do they use that bargaining power to your detriment? If so, how can you increase your standing? Are their prices increasing disproportionately to other business costs? If so, how do they explain this? How would you describe your relationship with them? Are they unique in their supply or are there alternative sources? Who do your competitors source from?

Substitutes

Is there anyone coming into the market offering something that could satisfy the same needs that you are, but in a better, more efficient, more enjoyable, in fact better all round manner? See these people as competitors. If a customer is not spending money with you, where else could they be spending it? If you are running a small riding school which targets the social, fun rider rather than the serious competitive sportsperson, you must consider what substitute companies are doing to lure the customers' Sunday money away. What are swimming pools and leisure centres doing? What about the local ice rink? What about mountain bike, sailing and walking clubs? What about new activities such as off-road motorised vehicles, paint ball and cross-country assault courses? Little wonder many horse-riding establishments have moved into offering pub rides to compete with the substitutes.

Distributors

If you use distributors, how effective are they? Who are key? Are there other routes to the end customer you should be considering? How well are they representing you in the market? Do they favour your competitors? How important are you to them? Do they see your product as differentiated? Do they provide regular business? Are they able to source similar to your offer? What benefits do you provide them to represent your products to the end customer? It is very important for your salespeople to understand just how much of their business you are influencing.

Political trends

Imagine the threat to you as a manufacturer of petrol-driven lawnmowers if the government was trying to legislate to replace all petrol-driven tools with electricity-driven to protect the environment. You need to prepare and plan for getting out of the area if the law gets passed, getting expertise quickly in electricity-driven mowers, or forming an alliance with an electrical company. Imagine the opportunity to you as a manufacturer of electricity-driven tools if the same law gets passed. You would need to plan how you intend to capture the new custom.

Economic trends

Here you should be considering things such as interest rates, inflation, unemployment, strength of sterling and so on. These can have a huge impact on your business and on different segments of the marketplace. Imagine that 80 per cent of your business is currently abroad. Now imagine that because of the strength of the pound your pricing shoots up by 80 per cent – you are now too expensive compared to local providers because of exchange rates. Likewise, imagine you are a small gift retailer selling British souvenirs to American and Japanese holidaymakers. Or a small guesthouse operating as a B & B to foreign visitors in the Lake District. In the summer of 2000 the strength of the pound proved to be a real problem for many small businesses such as these – the UK became too expensive as a holiday destination and visitors stayed away in their droves. Coupled with the strong pound making it extremely cheap to visit continental Europe, this economic trend posed great threats to UK businesses in this market place. If this threat is apparent then what are you going to do to get business?

Social trends

Ultimately all market demand derives itself from the spending power of people. Have their tastes changed? Is the teenage market shrinking as a percentage of the UK population? What opportunities does the increasing numbers of over 50s, the so-called grey market provide? Think how the attitudes to life are changing – some old people are young at heart while others may be happy to be old. Is the current trend one of conspicuous consumption (labels to prove my wealth) or minimalist chic? Does the fact that Jeremy Clarkson wears Levi's make them too uncool for the teenagers? What percentage of the population is using the Internet? How many people are increasingly working from home and therefore need home office space? Fail to monitor changing demographics, habits, lifestyles and tastes and you will lose out. Is the segmentation of the market changing in a way that makes your target definition out-dated and irrelevant – is age, for example, still the key determinant of differing needs in your market, or is the presence of children in the household more relevant?

In March 2001 it was announced that the percentage of the UK population with £50 000 liquid assets (cash, savings) was the highest it had ever been. But before all the luxury goods and sports car manufacturers see this as a great opportunity and rub their hands with glee, the announcement went on to say that these wealthy individuals were not at all motivated by conspicuous consumption of labels and materialistic goods. They are much more likely to be looking to spend their money on lifestyle improvements

– leisure, relaxation and health. So all businesses in these markets can harness the opportunity.

Technological trends

The speed of technological change is a real threat for companies that fail to keep up with developments, but creates opportunities for those that do. If you are a management training provider, the boom of the Internet and improvements in interactive learning technology could have a huge impact on your business. As a small business you must be realistic about your need for technology compared to your large global competitors. Competitive advantage does not come from having the technology, but from knowing how to use it. For example, the supermarkets' introduction of loyalty cards giving points and ultimately money off for every £ spent in-store progressed from being a technique to encourage loyalty to becoming a tool to gather information about customers. They wanted to know everything about you by tracking your purchasing habits through the point-of-sale data and data stored on the magnetic strip on the card. It was some time before the super-markets were skilled enough to know what to do with this information – to use it to speak to you as an individual and provide offers on products it knows interest you. All this did was replicate what it thought small corner shops were already doing – knowing the customer personally in order to be better at satisfying their needs. So the learning here for a small corner shop would have been about the trend towards supermarkets speaking to people more personally using technology – a threat to the personal relationships they had with customers and therefore the need to ensure their customer service and care was up to scratch.

Legal trends

Before opening your launderette business check to see if there is any legislation in the pipeline relating to machines used – perhaps there are proposals being considered around minimising detergent releases into drains. If the legislation is passed, will your machines be within regulation? If legislation states that all part-time workers must have four weeks' paid annual leave, what is the impact on your staffing levels? If you are importing or exporting, ensure you remain on top of changing legislation in the foreign countries you deal with – imagine the threat if the government were to add 25 per cent import duty to the cost of your goods. Consider the opportunities that may exist in other markets where heavy lobbying has opened the market to your offer.

Environmental trends

What will be the impact on the costs of running your café should it become a requirement for all toilets to operate on economy flush, all delivery vehicles to operate on low emission engines, all takeaway cups and plates to be recyclable, and all menus to be printed on recycled paper? Sadly and rather more topically, reflect on the devastating impact that the foot and mouth outbreak of March 2001 has had on every business related to agriculture or tourism. While some of the trends and happenings are things that can be anticipated and planned for, some are not. Some threats will arise that you can do absolutely nothing about – thankfully they are less common than those you can plan to deal with before they happen.

THE IMPORTANCE OF MONITORING TRENDS

If you operate a business dealing only in the Manchester area then ensure you focus on PESTLE trends within that area specifically, as well as national trends that may be influencing local ones. The percentage of the population above 55 may be growing in the UK, but is that the case in your local area?

The Swiss watch industry totally failed to monitor trends and developments in both the social and technological areas of their business. They made high-quality, extremely accurate, long-lasting, classic timepieces, but failed to recognise the emergence of a growing demand for less expensive more fashionable time-telling accessories. Coupled with new Japanese digital technology making the reduction of costs of manufacture and styling possible, the Swiss lost much in the battle for watch sales. When they did respond it was impressive – with Swatch – but they lost many years ground by failing to monitor trends.

Hamleys of Regent Street in London is a famous toy store. It has been around since long before the Disney and Warner Brother stores of recent years. Recently they have faced major financial troubles as they failed to keep up with kids' changing tastes for toys. Children don't just want toys; they want lifestyle accessories. Would it shock you to hear that only 2 per cent of Hamleys stock was dedicated to electronic toys?

The BMW brand has suffered slightly in the UK as patriotic supporters of and workers at Rover cars were dismayed at the handling of its disposal by BMW. Rover cars were suffering from expensive UK manufacturing costs relative to foreign manufacture, higher than average sale prices and a general lack of differentiation in the market in UK – the customer target was unclear, and people just weren't too sure why they should buy a Rover; being owned by BMW it wasn't British anymore, it wasn't the sexiest, it wasn't most stylish, it wasn't most fashionable, it wasn't best made in the customers' eyes. Rover was purchased in June 2000 by ex-Rover managers determined to turn the company around. If their fortunes are to improve, they must keep an external focus. A BBC news reporter asked the new management team why they will now see a turnaround in fortunes – not once did the spokesperson mention the need to give customers a reason to buy the Rover brand. He spoke instead of internal manufacturing brilliance and committed staff. Yes, these are key requirements, but only if customers want to buy your product. By early 2001 the new Rover group were still struggling to make a profit. As soon as you stop satisfying customers then you must do something to change – Rover and the likes must remain externally focused if they are to do this.

Anita and Gordon Roddick are famous for their Body Shop – the store based on concern for the environment offering face and body care products made from natural ingredients and packaged in environmentally friendly recyclable containers. However, this was not their first business venture. In the early 1970s they opened a

Example PESTLE analysis

	Trend	Opportunity/threat
Political	Increase to minimum wage	Increased wage bill reduces margins
	Reduced university places	Graduate recruiters will face more competition
Economic	Strong pound	Threat to foreign sales, need to assess new markets
Social	Increasing spending on eating out	Opportunity to open coffee shop in evening as restaurant
	Graduates wish to work more in e-commerce businesses	Graduate recruiters need to acquire new skills and client base
Technological	Internet usage increasing among target market	Take restaurant bookings over Internet
	Increasing penetration of Internet at university	Use Internet to find candidates and match skills with client places
Legal	No building on out of town sites	Warehouse locations?
Environmental	Growing concern over green issues	Extend range of natural products offered

little vegetarian restaurant, supporting the same healthy, natural, green issues as the Body Shop, but the restaurant failed – the Roddicks opened the restaurant for internal not external reasons, the market was not ready at that time for vegetarian food. The Roddicks liked the idea, but failed to check if any customers would respond positively. Based on an understanding of their environment they changed their menu and approach to suit the mood of the time and were soon running a successful American-style hamburger joint. They waited until 1976 to open their first Body Shop.

There is a lesson here for many of the dotcom businesses who have disappeared already (dotbombs they're being called): don't start a business for your own reasons without checking out the customer need. Think carefully about PESTLE for your business. It should be a task you think about frequently, depending on the dynamics of the market in which you are competing. Remember that the key is not just identifying the trend, but clarifying what is the potential opportunity or threat to your business. To be honest, it doesn't matter whether you talk about changes in drink-driving legislation as a political or legal trend, or the minimum wage as a political or a legal trend – the point is that you at least consider it and the potential opportunity or threat. So PESTLE is not a theoretical handcuff, but just a helpful tool to ensure you try to consider everything that might be relevant.

I read a quote once which said, 'there are three types of companies – those who make things happen, those who watch things happen and those who wonder what happened'. In failing to monitor your external environment you will become one of those who '. . . wonder what happened'. In order to be one of those who 'make things happen' you've got to monitor the external environment and then actually do something about it! You've got to use external understanding internally – use it to drive the direction of your actions. Use it to drive the direction of *all* of your actions: actions that Chapter 4 will explore.

USING EXTERNAL
UNDERSTANDING INTERNALLY

Being externally focused allows you to be internally strong. How?

1. By knowing which are the key opportunities and threats you are going to deal with in the future it allows you to plan how to compete. It allows you to identify and prioritise skills and resources you must develop if you are to take full advantage of these opportunities and threats.
2. By knowing where your strengths and weaknesses lie compared to the competition it allows you to develop and utilise the required internal skills and resources. If your delivery service is a real weakness in your operation, you know you have to improve upon it. If your customer service is a real strength compared to the competition, plan to make the most of it.
3. External understanding will become the driver of your business strategy – how you will achieve competitive advantage, how you will satisfy customers better than competitors, profitably.

An easy approach to using your external focus to drive your strategy is as follows:

- identify trends in your environment
- determine the main opportunities and threats to your business posed by these trends
- clarify your strengths and weaknesses compared to competitors
- map out things in your business to keep doing, improve and change.

Potentially there is so much information that you can gather in the process of using external focus to drive your strategy. Before we look at how to go about gathering the relevant information I'd like to consider first how to make it useful to you once collected. Unless the mass of data and information is put into a practical and manageable format, it will stay as a mass of data. It will be lengthy, repetitive, cumbersome, unprioritised, unfocused and as a result ineffective. You will find it hard to develop strategy and actions from such data.

This is where a SWOT analysis comes into its own. A SWOT analysis stands for Strengths, Weaknesses, Opportunities and Threats analysis.

SWOT ANALYSIS

This tool captures the strengths and weaknesses of your business in the marketplace, and the opportunities and threats facing it from the external environment.

By using the template in the SWOT analysis table opposite, you have all the important issues facing you on one or two sheets of paper. If you have yet to put together a business plan, you may find SWOT analysis to be one of the most useful things you can do. I guarantee it's one of the first things that any bank or financial institution or business angel will turn to. It will instantly display:

Principles of a SWOT analysis

Strengths	Weaknesses
■ Important things you have which competitors don't ■ Things you do better than competitors ■ Things you must keep doing	■ Things you do worse than your competitors ■ Important things you lack versus the competition ■ Things you must improve (or find customers who don't value them)

Opportunities	Threats
■ Areas the business can and should should attack ■ Identified in external environment needs ■ Focus on attractive opportunities ■ Focus on opportunities to which competitors are less able to respond	■ Areas to which you must respond ■ Identified in external environment trends ■ Focus on threats likely to occur and serious ■ Ignore at your peril

■ whether you have a real understanding of the dynamics of the market
■ whether you have an objective view of who you are competing against
■ whether your strategy is based on solid assumptions.

So to get from the mass of data to the one or two page document you need to:

■ gather the information (see the next section for detail on how to do this)
■ integrate and organise the data into sections
■ prioritise the key information (you don't have resource or time to deal with all opportunities, look to the key ones)
■ be objective (do not pretend to have no weaknesses, and do not overestimate your strengths)
■ be customer focused (focus on strengths that are important to customers or important things that will help satisfy customers). Do not concentrate time and money fixing things which will have no impact on the customer perception or success of your business – by all means be aware of any issues but don't lose focus.

If we go back to the Hamleys example; they need to understand their strengths and weaknesses compared to other toy retailers, how customers' tastes have changed, what the different opportunities and threats to their business continue to be. From this SWOT analysis they would be in a position to decide clearly what sort of retailer they want to be, which customer segment(s) they wish to target, and what the new offer will be to satisfy these customers better than competitors. This is being externally focused and internally strong.

HOW TO GET THE
INFORMATION YOU NEED

You'll have gathered by this stage that there's quite a lot of work goes into being externally focused and completing a SWOT analysis. In order to get answers or at least an idea of the trends and changes and perceptions in the market then you really become a market researcher. This is not as formal or theoretical as it sounds – much of the information is to be gained by informal means: keeping your eyes and ears open, reading the newspaper, listening to the radio, networking with people.

In addition to the informal (but really important) routes mentioned above, there are broadly three ways to monitor your environment:

1. Desk research
2. Field research of competitors
3. Field research of customers (current and potential).

1. Desk research

Desk research is exactly what it says; research you do at a 'desk': at home, in a library, from books, over the Internet, from published research reports, from magazines, newspapers and journals and so on. Desk research should be your first port of call before rushing out to interview customers or competitors or industry experts – it will save you quite a bit of time, money and hassle as somewhere the answers to your questions may already exist.

Where to find desk research information

Libraries

- Your nearest reference library
- Any specialist business library
- Library of a local college that runs business courses.

Beware! In a good library the quantity of information available is massive. So try to have a list of specific answers you are looking for. Go to the librarian and ask to be pointed in the right direction. Do not present a huge long list of questions but focus on two or three key points, as you will find that one thing tends to lead to another. You might find that a market report on growth of eating out in the UK mentions an article about leading companies who will be your competitors – so find this article.

The type of information ranges from the general to the specific; published market reports or articles in back issues of journals will give a good overview of your market and trends. Government statistics on household expenditure might answer more specific questions. Some reports may concentrate solely on social trends in your market.

So rule number 1 is – before you look for anything know what specifically you want answers to. General directories will give information on competitors or customers:

- *Retail Trade UK*
- *Computer Users Yearbook* (cssonline.co.uk)
- *BT Directory*
- *Yellow Pages*
- *Thomson Local* (thomsonlocal.co.uk)
- *Kelly's Manufacturers and Merchant's Directory* (kellys.co.uk)
- *Dun and Bradstreet* (dunandbrad.co.uk)
- *Kompass Register UK* (kompassregister.co.uk)
- *Directory of British Associations* (britishcompanies.co.uk).

Statistical information will help with social and economic trends (see the government website):

■ Guide to Official Statistics
■ Monthly Digest of Statistics
■ Annual Abstract of Statistics
■ Business Monitors
■ Overseas Trade Statistics
■ Living in Britain
■ Census and Census Projections
■ National Food Survey
■ Employment Gazette
■ Regional Trends
■ National Income and Expenditure Blue Book.

The following companies give information on specific markets, trends, competitors and customers, legislation, etc., in published Market Research Reports:

■ ICC Keynote (eins.org)
■ Datamonitor (datamonitor.com)
■ Market Research Great Britain
■ Mintel (sintra2.mintel.com)
■ Economist Intelligence Unit (eiu.com)
■ Canadean (drinks markets) (canadean.com).

Find which reports exist by looking at indexes of Market Research Reports: Marketsearch, MSI Marketing Surveys index or libraries own indexes. These reports can cost thousands to buy – so find a good reference library or business library.

For information relating to advertising publications and costs, competitor spend on advertising and anything related to reaching customers or trends socially try:

■ European Marketing Data and Statistics
■ The A–Z of UK Marketing Data
■ BRAD (British Rate and Data)
■ MEAL (Media Expenditure Analysis Limited).

In the past newspapers or journals may have featured relevant articles. Have a search for such articles using:

- McCarthy News on CD Rom (key word search)
- F&S Index International
- British Humanities Index
- Prediscast Europe.

Internet

As with a library, and probably even more so due to having no librarian to ask, the internet is a potentially vast and confusing source of information. There is, however, an article on how to do research on the Internet that has linked sites:

www.wmin.ac.uk/~bradlen/papers/tour.html

In browsing a topic it's probably best to look at a directory – a group of sites related by a common theme, e.g. music, property, loft living, leisure clubs, etc. and range from the obvious to the most obscure topics. Yahoo! is a directory as are Lycos.com, Excite.com, and Britannica.com.

Search engines are popular for the serious researcher. They investigate topics across all directories and in gathering specific data from a range of sites, present it to you on a single page! In his *Rough Guide to the Internet*, Angus Kennedy says, 'Once you've tried Copernic.com you'll never want to use an individual search engine again'.

Don't forget Reuters, the *Financial Times*, and any relevant industry bodies. On registering with them you will receive daily/weekly/updates of issues in the industry. They can be found at FT.com and Reuters.com.

Banks

Now I know this may sound surprising, but the bank where your business account is located may be a great source of information.

Barclays, for example, offer (soon to be online if not so already) market information bulletins that will give you information about specific markets, mainstream and niche (fishing flies should you so wish) and business information bulletins (for example 'How to write a press release').

Despite your search, this published information may not answer every question you have. As a small business you are likely to be so unique or specialised in some way that it is unlikely for precise answers to your questions to exist already. You may have to gather useful data personally. Your own field research will also involve speaking with or observing competitors and customers.

2. Competitor field research

How do you find out how they run their operation and what their views of the trends in the market are? How do you assess their strengths and weaknesses? Well there are several devious, and less so approaches:

- pretend to be a customer (or get someone to do it for you) to assess their performance and evaluate their response
- interview an experienced owner of a competitive business, someone willing to share his or her experiences and thoughts
- visit your competitors' shops, cafés, websites, etc.; visit their offices if you can, get hold of their literature, experience their offer
- talk to your competitors' customers.

These are all examples of field research, or primary research. Where desk research involved finding reports and information ready printed or documented from past work by others, field research means going out there and getting your own answers to your own questions. Interview your competitors face to face, send a questionnaire through the mail or over the Internet, call them up over the telephone, observe them at work or in action – all are ways to get the information you need. Only by detailed and objective analysis of all your competitors' strengths and weaknesses can you really assess your ability to compete effectively.

What you might want to ask them face to face

I know you're probably thinking why on earth would my competitor help me out? But they could be someone you used to work with in the past, a contact through a friend or someone who operates in a different location to you. Alternatively someone who works in a similar if not identical business could help you, e.g. if you are selling graphic design and can't interview another graphic designer, speak to a different professional service provider. If you are opening a gift shop, try a different sort of shop. Explain that you will need about 45 minutes of their time. Identify clearly what the purpose of your information gathering is. Before you prepare a short list of questions be absolutely clear what you want to know.

This research can be really effective in helping you determine what you really need to be good at, what customers' expectations in the market are, how customers responded in the past to certain competitive offers, experiences competitors had with certain strategies, the changes they anticipate in the future, which of their competitors they fear, see as vulnerable and why?

3. Customer field research

This is probably the most important research and information gathering you do. You want current and potential customers to give you an idea of how satisfied they are at present with offers from both you and your competitors, specific things you do well, critical things the customer expects you to do and get right, how the customer perceives your offer compared to competitors, problems the customer has at the moment, how they think their requirements may change in the future, solutions to problems they look for but can't find and so on. This is done by every business, large and small.

Imagine you are the owners of Concorde, which has since its creation in the 1970s had such a great image. Concorde crashed in

France in July 2000 killing all the passengers and crew. The impact of that crash on the image of Concorde must be considered if they are to still fly daily – do customers now perceive the plane to be too unsafe, will loyal passengers enjoying a four-hour transatlantic flight sacrifice time for safety, will people still wish to take two hour trips to Cornwall and back in order to say they have experienced the thrill of breaking the speed of sound?

There are various routes to gathering customer information. Big companies employ research specialist agencies on their behalf to carry out sophisticated and extremely expensive customer analysis. Focus groups, household shopping behaviour tracking, national surveys, shopper observation, accompanied shopping trips, psychological profiling – the list goes on. For your business (to add to the trend information you have gathered from your desk research) there are a couple of key techniques you can use that are cost and time effective and give just as accurate results:

- surveys/questionnaires (by phone, by post, on internet)
- personal interviews (face to face)
- observation.

Of course much of the valuable information you can gain about your customers – current, ex-, loyal, prospect – will come from simply keeping your eyes and ears open: speaking to them informally day to day, seeing them in your place of business, what they say to you and your staff. Big companies envy your closeness to your market – take hold of this advantage.

Let me cover the observation technique first. It involves the observation and noting of customer behaviour while shopping for or using products and services. As these activities tend to be habitual and automatic, customers find it difficult to recall and verbalise what they do, therefore normal questionnaires and inter-views are not the best way to gain information. You are not going to get the reasons why people behave the way they do, but you are in a position to see the reality – Mrs Harvie may say she always buys organic fruit and vegetables, but by observing you will see the truth. You will be able to see how long people take to make a purchase decision, how they react when approached by a sales representative, how they behave when the outlet is busy or quiet and so on. Just make sure you're not too obvious with your spying.

One large global organisation who manufactures and sells and range of consumer products: household, food, health and beauty, wanted information on working-class customers in India to help plan their advertising campaigns. They assumed, and had it confirmed by desk research, that the percentage of the population owning a television set was very small. They therefore chose to advertise on radio as they'd heard that workers took a radio to the fields as company throughout the working day. It was only by visiting these people and observing them across a typical week, getting insight into their real lives, did the company discover key facts. Not only did the workers chat over the radio speaking to each other all day at work, but that once or twice a week an entire village would congregate and out would be wheeled the village pride and joy – a television set. The village would devour an evening of 'Bollywood' films, soaps and advertising – it was a form of escapism, romanticism, but also a link with the outside world. It was using observation as a means of gathering information that identified the opportunity of television advertising for the company.

Some companies, such as airlines, supermarkets and bookstores, use another type of observation technique to assess how well they are doing: mystery shoppers. People posing as real customers go to the store, through check-in procedures, on board, telephone customer service so they can experience what the customer experiences. It stops the 'smelling of paint' syndrome – the Queen thinks the whole world smells of fresh paint because everything's been cleaned up and painted before she arrives; she never sees the reality.

Surveys and personal interviews, of course, rely on you questioning respondents. Survey and questionnaires will typically involve lots of yes/no, box-ticking type questions and take less time than a personal interview that will tend to require lots of open questions and long comment style answers.

I hope the following guidelines are helpful:

1. Do not ask questions for the sake of it. People generally do not like being questioned.

Face-to-face, telephone or postal survey research

	Pros	Cons
Face-to-face interviews	Flexibility and control Can prompt with visuals Can clarify misunderstanding Can watch body language	Time consuming People cynical of being stopped in street Where to do interview
Telephone	Convenient if customers are national Good for business customers used to using telephones Instant feedback	Must be short Intrusive for customers At a convenient time
Postal	Respondent can complete when it suits them	Extremely low response rate Very slow to receive replies Which member of the household completed it?

2. Therefore be crystal clear what you want to know.
3. Make it as easy and unobtrusive as possible for people to answer.
4. Get a good range of people who typically represent your customers and prepare to question them.
5. Consider offering them an incentive for helping you? Money off their next purchase? A free head massage next time they come for a haircut? Two coffees for the price of one? Anything to thank them for their help.

Deciding how to conduct your survey is another matter and is up to you based on your budget, time constraints and the pros and cons of each, as shown in the table above.

An example of competitor and customer research

In Chapter 1 I mentioned Artizian Catering Services, who make eating in the office canteen an exciting experience. Key to their success has been the adoption of high-street eating trends into their contracted restaurants. They try to stay ahead of the latest trends, too, by finding out what is happening in the USA and bringing those ideas to the United Kingdom (coffee and nail bars have spawned from US success). The chefs are also charged with eating out to learn what the competition are up to and what new trends in eating are emerging, and all managers in the business must find out about local eating alternatives for canteen users.

In the following section we will provide some tips should you wish to put together a questionnaire to survey your market.

PUTTING TOGETHER A RESEARCH SURVEY/QUESTIONNAIRE

1. Always start with easy questions that are quick to answer.
2. If you really need to know sensitive information such as someone's age or income, give them ranges to choose from, i.e. 16–25, 26–35, £12 000–£25 000 per year.
3. Don't use jargon – make it easy to understand – or people will make up an answer if they feel too embarrassed to say they don't understand.
4. Don't use words that are easy to misinterpret. If you ask someone whether they use the Internet frequently, how will they interpret frequently? To a heavy user frequently may mean twice per day, and to my mother may mean once a fortnight.
5. Give options to choose from: every day/twice per week/once per week/weekends only.
6. Asking someone if they like your offer is a fairly useless question. They are likely to say yes in order to please you, but may not be willing to explain why. 'Like' is another hard to interpret word. Instead, ask someone what in particular he or she enjoys about dealing with you/what you could improve upon.
7. Don't ask too many questions (particularly in a questionnaire you mail to people). There is a time beyond which you try their patience (around 10 minutes). Longer than that you risk them not completing it and therefore not returning it, completing it rashly with false information or, worse, giving it to someone else to complete for them.

8. Don't leave the really important questions to the end – they may have switched off by then.
9. Beware too many 'why' or 'please explain' questions. People do get bored writing and may feel they couldn't possibly explain their thoughts and feelings in words anyhow. These questions are perhaps best left for face-to-face interviews.

SUMMARY CHECKLIST

- If the market changes, so should you
- If you don't know what your strengths are, why should a customer
- Monitor your environment to identify the key opportunities and threats you must or could respond to
- A SWOT analysis is a good start point for your strategy – it summarises what the strengths and weaknesses of your business are and the key opportunities and threats facing it
- Information gathering takes time – know what you want to find out before you begin
- Keeping your eyes and ears open is as helpful in identifying trends as formal market research can be.

4

Getting Your Offer Right

The rewards in business go to the man who does something with an idea.
William Benton

THE CHAPTER AT A GLANCE

So by now you are clear about the opportunities that exist, the threats to deal with, the strengths you need to build on and perhaps key weaknesses to address in order to satisfy customers. You clearly understand the consumers/customers you will target. You are clear that you have the skills and requirements to satisfy these people better than any competitors are doing or could do. You know there is a chance that your idea could succeed. You are now ready to turn the idea into a great 'offer'. An 'offer' is the totality of everything you do and deliver to customers that will satisfy them consistently and hopefully encourage their loyalty. It's everything they experience when dealing with you. We will now look at the elements that make up the offer as a whole.

This chapter is the first of many to focus on those parts of the marketing iceberg above the surface – the tactics of marketing (see Chapter 1). Thinking creatively will ensure that your tactics grab and hold your target customers' attentions. Copying your competitors is a bit of a cop out really. You have a great opportunity to be different from the competition and better than anyone else at satisfying your customers' differing needs.

WHAT WE MEAN BY AN 'OFFER'

Your offer is the totality of everything you do, everything customers experience when dealing with you. If you have a shop, it's the physical products or services you sell, the name over the door, the layout and style of the store, the prices you charge, the staff you have, the services you offer, the way you handle complaints and the way you advertise and communicate your store. If you have a factory, it's the products you make, the prices you charge, the way you package, the delivery process to customers, the stores you sell to, the salespeople and staff you have, your refund and complaints policies, and the manner in which you communicate with potential and current customers to keep them buying.

While it is this 'totality' you need to get right, it might be helpful to split it into, and think more about, the elements that make up the total offer. These elements are commonly known as the *marketing mix*:

- product or service core
- price
- distribution
- communication
- people/customer service.

A great offer is one that is consistent across each of the elements of the mix.

A quick and dirty example: if you are operating a laundry or dry cleaning shop, offering varied services from basic dry cleaning up to specialist services, shirt pressing, wedding dress cleaning and delicates care, then make sure your shop is clean. If you are an upmarket gift shop, make sure the way you package customers' purchases reflects this. If you are an expensive restaurant, make sure you offer surroundings reinforcing the expense. If you are a beautician with a beauty salon, make sure your staff look clean, tidy and not a stranger to the service you are providing. Boots the Chemist are great advocates of this – right down to the delivery trucks you see driving around the country; the trucks must be washed and clean. Boots know that positioning themselves as a Health and Beauty store means everything must look beautiful.

You may have great ads, great prices, great showrooms and sales assistants, but what happens when a potential customer gets cut up on the motorway by rude driving (accompanied by digit signalling) of a vehicle blazoned with your name, logo and telephone number?

'How am I driving?' is a classic example of businesses recognising that marketing means satisfaction at every potential moment of interaction with a customer, current or potential. You can have a great product, but if it is always out of stock when people come to buy then you have failed. You can have a great advert that draws people to your decorating service, but if you promise to start on Monday morning and be finished within two weeks but don't turn up until Wednesday and take six weeks to do the job, it's unlikely you will have satisfied the customers, and unlikely that he or she will recommend you to anyone else.

ELEMENTS OF THE OFFER

Core product or service

Whether it's physical products or services you are providing be clear what constitutes the core elements. What will the packaging look like? What sizes will you provide? What is the range you will offer? Do you provide after-sales service? What about guarantees and warranties? Are parts available? What logo and signage will you have?

Price

What is the price you will charge for your product or service? What will your discount policy be? What credit terms will you offer? How will you charge for extra services you may offer? What payment methods will you accept? What is your price policy if a customer cancels a booking?

Distribution/place

How do you get your offer to the customers? Where will you be based? What are your opening hours? What does your store, office or place of business look like? Do you deliver? How far do you deliver? What do you charge for delivery? When do you deliver? Will you sell through the Internet? Will you sell through mail-order brochures? Are you able to offer a speedier service in an emergency?

Communication

In other books on marketing this element is sometimes called promotion – how do you promote your business to customers new and old? I have changed the word as I feel that sometimes people translate the word promotion into 'bargain' or think of demonstrators in stores. By communication I mean how do you make people aware of your offer, how do you convince them it is better than any other, and then how do you make sure they buy? How do you tell them and what do you tell them? The choices open to you here are enormous –and you may find that budget is a big determinant.

People/customer service

How many will you have? How much knowledge and expertise can they offer? What roles do they have – answer phones, take orders, handle complaints, all or some? How will you offer outstanding customer service? What is your complaints handling policy? How do you deal with unhappy customers?

EXAMPLES OF CONSISTENT MARKETING MIX

Let's look at an example of a business that is consistent across each element of the mix. Animal is a company producing and selling a range of products aimed particularly at sporty/surfy/skateboardy types. 'Time to Ride' is a phrase they use. Have a look at their great website www.animal.co.uk. They produce watches, luggage, accessories and clothing. The watches are sporty and hard wearing, the luggage is casual rucksacks, bum bags and holdalls. The accessories are casual caps, wallets, belts, watch straps, stickers and water bottles. The clothing is both technical for sports people (snowboard jackets and pants and wet suits) and urban for everyday wear. They sell through surfing, skateboard and snow and ski board stores and sailing, jet-ski and water-ski parks – never in high street jewellers or stores. They sponsor alternative action sports – surfing and boarding, use top surfers to endorse their clothing, and lobby with the Surfers Against Sewage group against sea pollution. The watches are sporty looking, have different coloured faces, a range of interchangeable fabric straps in modern colourful designs, velcro fastening for easy removal, completely waterproof and packaged in durable, recycled cardboard, dome-shaped boxes carrying their distinctive logo. The company offers a complete repair service of all parts throughout the guarantee period and beyond.

Holmes Place Gym also demonstrates consistency across the marketing mix:

■ Product	– swimming pool, gymnasium, exercise/aerobics studios, crèche, restaurant offering healthy meals, luxury changing rooms with shampoo, towels, body lotion. etc.
■ Price	– in line with premium sports and leisure clubs fully inclusive monthly fee offers for local businesses
■ Distribution	– modern facilities, long opening hours, working professionals' catchment areas
■ Communication	– TV ads, local newspaper ads, recommend a friend schemes
■ People/customer service	– high staff/member ratio, fully qualified and experienced in exercise/fitness/gym, personal trainers available, ability to test fitness levels and chart progress, regular programme updates, motivational assistance, suggestion schemes, respond immediately to customer feedback.

Both companies focus on ensuring their entire 'experience' will interest, attract, satisfy and retain customers.

The marketing mix gives you potential to offer a great experience to customers. The satisfaction and delight in dealing with a business will be as a result of what you experience at a particular moment in time. This experience can be made up of things you see, perceive, hear, touch and smell. The experience you offer can keep you ahead of the game. Competitors can sell similar products to you at similar prices and can advertise in similar places and deliver by similar means and have customer service operators on the end of a telephone 24 hours a day – just like you. However, what they cannot compete with is the manner in which you put it all together into a customer experience that helps you stay the supplier of choice.

HOW TO DEVELOP AN OFFER

In the main, three things will help you develop an offer and experience to keep you ahead of the game:

1. Target customer understanding and insight.
2. Competitor understanding and insight.
3. Clearly knowing what you want to stand for.

Points 1 and 2 are I suppose obvious. (You will have realised by now that most of marketing is common sense.)

The target customer

Remember that in Chapter 2 we said that the single most important thing you can spend time doing is clearly defining your target market – all offer decisions come from knowing who they are, where they live, their tastes, their real needs and so on. You can't make decisions about the menu, prices, décor, location, communication and service in your coffee shop (your marketing mix) until you are clear about your target market. Animal find it easy to develop a clear and consistent marketing mix offer because they have a clear understanding of the precise customer they are targeting; think alternative 'surfy'-types – both actual and aspirational.

Imagine you are an Independent Financial Adviser (IFA). Within your database of customers you may have four different segments whom you are targeting.

1. The *comfortable and contented* family with few money worries who need sound financial advice to protect and build their investment portfolio.
2. The *up and coming* individual who tries to understand and actively manage their finances, but needs some help with the fine tuning of decisions.
3. The *habit bound* single or couple who don't like risk, don't have much spare cash, so need to guarantee income in the short to mid-term.
4. *Busy professionals* who need, want, you to be proactive, as they don't have time to keep a tight control on their financial position as their personal circumstances change.

If you are going to satisfy the needs of each of these segments then the offer for each of the segments will be slightly different, maybe some elements will be constant, but the detail will be different. Otherwise why have you gone to the effort of trying to understand the differing needs of the segments in the first place?

So let's take the segment that wants you to be proactive, the *busy professional*: what will your offer to them comprise, your offer to satisfy their needs?

- As each tax year-end approaches why not contact them showing them how they haven't, yet could, take advantage of the tax allowances for the year. Suggest where their money could go that will avoid payment of tax.
- Regularly suggest a review to check that current investments are still relevant, performing well and of the right type for the individual. Has their financial position changed? Have their objectives changed? Have their circumstances changed?
- If you know the individual has to complete a tax return for the year declaring gross personal pension contributions, calculate

the figure for them. Send them a note saying, 'I hope this will save you time and hassle, here's the figure for box 21A on your tax return. It comes from the following calculation'.

■ Send out a quarterly newsletter (no need to be expensively glossy), telling the customers of all the recent happenings and changes in the financial world – what the changes mean to you as a saver/investor. Cover government budget regulation, budget news, scare stories from the general press and media.

■ If you have an Internet site, have a question and answer page.

■ Attract new busy professionals who have no time to meet you, by visiting them in their place of work over lunch.

These are just a few ideas for your marketing mix for this segment. There are some things in your marketing mix which may be common to all customers (a minimum level of service, a typical range of services you offer, etc.). As a business you can stay ahead of the game by tailoring your standard marketing mix to the specific needs of target market customers as shown above for the busy professional.

If you do none of this, you run the danger of giving the impression that you've got the business and you simply don't care anymore – you've moved onto the next customer. Remember basic marketing principles: it's cheaper and more profitable to look after the customers you have than to keep getting new ones. I know you don't want to be a pest and give the impression you are just trying to sell another policy, but remember the segmentation. This segment wants you to be proactive. Always look to see where you can add value to each segment and customer – delight and amaze him or her.

But try to think and plan with some degree of caution. There is a fine line between tailoring an offer for a segment and incurring unnecessary costs in the process in areas that really will not be perceived as making a difference to the customer, or that the customer will never notice. I hear the argument hundreds of times in large companies: 'the stick of the ice creams has to be different because the customers are different', 'chicken soup in market X tastes different to that in market Y because customers expect it that way'. Is there really any need for 14 different specifications for the stick in an ice cream, or 37 different flavours of chicken soup? Think of the extra costs incurred in doing this – there is no way that the perceived value in an ice cream stick covers the costs of purchasing and using it. The differentiation and value in the ice cream does not come from the stick, and while customers never cease to amaze in how they perceive products and in sub-consciously what drives purchase, all you are doing is adding complexity to your business. Think carefully about the 80 : 20 rule. That 80 per cent of your business may be provided by 20 per cent of your customers, or that 80 per cent of your business comes from only 20 per cent of your products. Concentrate on getting total complete satisfaction in the 20 per cent of customers, and on the 20 per cent of the products you offer.

The competition

In addition to basing your marketing mix offer on the needs of your specific target market(s), you should also develop your offer based on how you can be different from and better than competitors. What will make customers buy from you rather than the com-petition? How will your experience be different for the customer? Perhaps the difference from the competition comes from the image you have – perhaps teenagers think you're trendier than the competition, perhaps men think your products are more masculine, perhaps parents think your products are safer for their children, perhaps drivers think your cars are sexier. This customer percep-tion, what you stand for in their mind, is the third key factor when developing your offer.

What you want to stand for

There is a quote I love which comes from *Alice in Wonderland*. She's lost in the forest and meets the Cheshire cat, and asks him: 'Which way should I go?' Upon which the cat replies: 'Well that depends on where you want to get to.'

The anomaly with marketing is that it's really helpful to have an idea about what you want to stand for before you try to develop your mix, otherwise you risk being inconsistent and confusing to the customer. Let me use some examples to explain this.

Which words come to mind when you think of:

- Coca-Cola?
- Pepsi?
- Virgin?
- Marlboro?

Let me share what I think. You may agree or disagree with my choice, but the words shown in the table above describe what the brands stand for in my mind.

A brand is a whole set of symbols, words, images and perceptions that determine what we believe that brand stands for. Marlboro wants to stand for American, rugged, outdoor, independent and classic. What a brand stands for is known as its 'positioning'.

Brand positioning – what your brand stands for in the mind of your customers, compared to the competition.

Knowing what you want to stand for, what positioning you want to have, will help you to develop your marketing mix offer.

WHAT YOU WANT TO STAND FOR – YOUR POSITIONING

There are many many books that deal solely with the topic of branding and positioning. I intend here only to skim the surface, and leave you to search the shelves of your library or bookshop should you wish to know more on the subject.

Positioning is about saying to customers, 'This is how I want you to perceive me', 'These are the benefits you can get from me' and 'These are the values that I stand for'.

What these brands may stand for

Coca-Cola	Pepsi	Virgin	Marlboro
Classic	New generation	Robin Hood	American
Traditional	Trendy	Quirky	Rugged
Red	Pop stars	Individual	Outdoor
American	Exciting		Cowboy
Always			Independent
			Classic

When choosing what you want your positioning to be, what you want to stand for, make sure it is:

- *relevant* to the target market
- *different* to the competition.

There is no point standing for cute and trendy and feminine if these values or benefits are not *relevant* to the target market. You may decide to stand for reliable, successful and considerate – but is this any *different* to what your competitors are saying? If not, why should customers come to you rather than the competition?

On knowing what your target customers' needs are, and on knowing what competitors are offering you may decide that you want to stand for quirky and individual/a 'Robin Hood'. This will help guide the tone and direction of every element of your marketing mix to ensure it is consistent.

Go back and look at the words I used to describe Coke versus Pepsi. From these positioning words alone (if you knew nothing else about the brands at all) which one would you choose to sponsor the Spice Girls? I'm not even going to insult you by telling you it's Pepsi – a clear example of positioning driving the communication element of your marketing mix.

Think about Volvo – what do think their positioning is – what do they stand for? I bet many of you said safety. Great. If you are a car manufacturer whose target market sees safety as a key benefit (functionally and emotionally) and if customers perceive that you make *the* car that provides this benefit better than anyone else, the target market is likely to prefer the Volvo brand. Now that you have

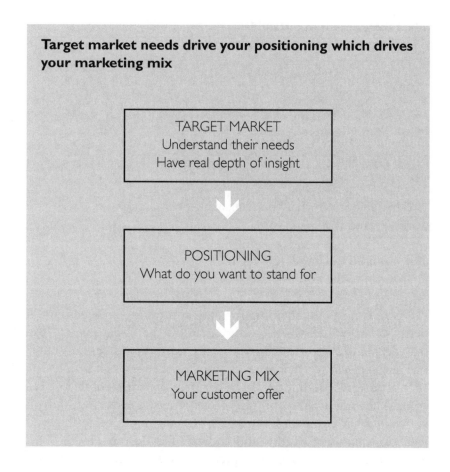

Target market needs drive your positioning which drives your marketing mix

safety as the key benefit that you offer customers, you must ensure that every element of your offer is in line with this: product design, pricing versus other models offering safety, your communication, the events you associate with, the places you sell your car.

Marlboro again – outdoor, American, cowboys, rugged, independence, freedom, strong, masculine are all words that describe the values of the brand. These words drive everything the brand does in its offer, ensuring consistency, in order to satisfy target customers.

■ Product – they would never make frilly and feminine clothing (all female clothing would probably look rugged and quite tomboyish) and they would never make their clothing in bright or pastel colours

- ■ Distribution – they would never sell in Woolworths or Asda, rather they sell in their own branded stores, as concessions in large department stores and at airport stores
- ■ Communication – they would never advertise in *Woman's Weekly* (unless it was a pattern on how to knit a Marlboro cowboy for your son!), they sponsor male dominated events such as Formula 1 motor racing
- ■ Pricing – premium in line with image

Pret a Manger, the upmarket 'sandwich' shop, which is located mainly in the south and in city centres is a great example of a business that is totally clear about what it stands for – this drives everything they do as a business – as even the carrier bag they provide says: 'We are passionate about food. Pret creates hand-made, natural food, avoiding the obscure chemicals, additives and preservatives common to so much of the "prepared" and "fast" food on the market today'. They make the sandwiches, baguettes and fresh salads in each store. 'We do not operate a central production factory nor employ mass production techniques. If our sandwiches don't sell out each day we give them away rather than compromise our standards.'

Positioning is very important in differentiating your offer – think about Nike and Adidas. Functionally both brands are pretty similar: sportswear and casual wear, high quality, fashionable, supportive where needed, sweat absorbing as required. The main difference between the brands comes in the emotional positioning – the image people perceive, the values that are relevant to the lives of some individuals. It is this image that can make a customer a staunch Nike fan or a loyal Adidas fan, or another customer buy one brand over another when all else is the same.

Be aware of the need to consider both functional and emotional benefits when positioning. Examples are shown in the table on the next page.

If you think about cars, a functional benefit is the ability to get from A to B as cheaply as possible, while an emotional benefit is the ability to prove to the other mothers at school when I'm dropping

Examples of functional and emotional benefits

Tangible (functional) benefits	Intangible (emotional) benefits
Long lasting	Masculine
Fuel efficient	Successful
Smooth	Trendy
Creamy	Youthful

off my son how successful my career is and how I can afford a gorgeous sporty car. Positioning can therefore be functional or emotional, but is usually a combination of the two.

If your positioning is completely functional (cheaper, faster, longer lasting, tastier, creamier), it makes it easy for a competitor to see where to copy your recipe for success. However, should your positioning also be emotional – if you can stand for something in customers' minds both tangibly and intangibly – it will be harder for competitors to copy or do it better.

The difficult thing about positioning is that while you may want to stand for one thing, customers could perceive something completely different. This may be because something in your marketing mix has caused this confused message, or perhaps because something completely outside your control has affected what your brand stands for.

Nescafé was the first instant coffee brand to be launched in the USA in the 1950s. The target market was the traditional housewife who currently spent a lot of time making fresh ground coffee. Nescafé wanted to stand for quickness and convenience, giving you time to do other more important things for your family. This positioning drove the Nescafé marketing mix, including television advertising. Unfortunately the target market interpreted the advertising to mean that you were lazy if you used the brand. Nescafé had to quickly alter their communication part of the mix.

Think about Hackett – the English clothing company. What do you think of? Words that used to spring to mind were traditionally English, rugby and polo. However, recently it seems to have become the uniform of football hooligans. Hackett are desperately trying to move away from this image.

So, please think carefully about your business and what you want to stand for. What will be the key benefits customers can get from

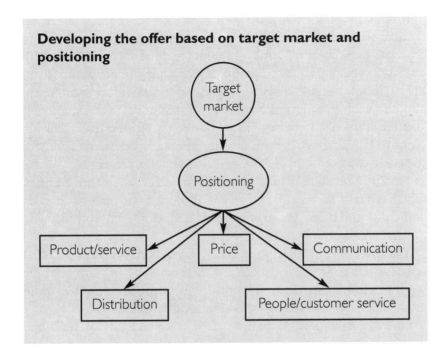

Developing the offer based on target market and positioning

you. How are you going to ensure that you will deliver against this promise? What will the elements of your marketing mix offer look like?

As the diagram above shows, by knowing your target market and what you want to stand for you can develop the different elements of the marketing mix into a consistent and integrated offer/experience for the customer.

We now move on to look in much more detail at the areas of product and service core, pricing, distribution, communication and people/customer service. To pricing, communication and people/customer service I've dedicated their own chapters. The following sections cover product and service core and distribution.

PRODUCT/SERVICE CORE

You must decide the range of products and services that comprise your offer to meet the needs of your customers, better than competitors, in line with your positioning.

If you are a beautician, do you offer everything from facials, to pedicures, from head to full body massages, from Thai massage to Swedish massage, from full make up to total face cleanse, from eyebrow tweezing to leg waxing and everything in between? If you are a window cleaner, do you just clean external windows or do you also clean the complete glazing of conservatories, inside and out? If you are a financial adviser, do you offer everything from pension plans to ISAs, from car insurance to life insurance, from tax advice to savings advice, from mortgages to annual tax returns? If you are in furniture retailing, which range do you offer? If you are a florist, which types of flowers do you sell? Will you sell pot-plants and vases and cards and bulbs and artificial flowers too? Or will you focus on arrangements and fresh cut flower sales?

This part of your offer is extremely important – as it says, it is the core of your entire physical offer. If the quality of the haircut or the window cleaning or the flowers or the furniture does not live up to expectations, the entire marketing mix can't redeem you.

One of the big supermarkets used to spend lots of time and money in developing a competitive marketing mix – value prices, wide range of products, baby changing facilities, delicatessen areas, ready-meal ranges, baby clubs, loyalty schemes, petrol stations, large trolleys for child comfort. However, they couldn't seem to get the core of their service right – availability on shelf. What good were baby changing facilities and a coffee shop if what you went to buy wasn't on the shelf? How long will it take before the customers stop giving them another chance to have goods in stock when they visit?

If you are retailing, you probably need to think about how your store looks, how the merchandise is displayed and how you will wrap the products. If you are manufacturing products then you will need to think about packaging for your products.

As part of this section on product/service core, let's look in more detail at the areas of packaging and merchandising/shop layout

Packaging

Packaging is especially important, as it may be the last thing at point of sale that the customer sees. Packaging is sometimes called the

'Silent Salesman'. It can help your products stand out against all the competition and remind about or prompt a purchase. It may be the last thing that attracts a passer-by into your store. You can use packaging to give the customer any information they may need to know (or any information that legally you must provide).

Packaging as the wrapping of a gift can reinforce the image of the product and packaging as the carrier bag from your outlet can signify an image (as well as being a communication vehicle for your outlet once the customer has left). I know of at least one irate customer (not sure I should admit to having such acquaintances) who went to Mappin & Webb jewellers to buy a Cartier watch. Everything about the watch and the service were perfect. But on exchanging his money for the watch he was handed not a Cartier branded bag, but one from Mappin & Webb. Not a huge problem on the scale of things you will agree, but certainly enough to deter him from making luxury purchases from there again. It comes down to having great customer insight I suppose. Selfridges department store in London is well aware of such insights – they even ensure that clothing such as Ralph Lauren is displayed on Ralph Lauren branded clothes hangers.

It is also important to get packaging right as it plays a practical and functional role in protecting any products inside. There are two things to be aware of in ensuring your packaging protects the contents: the cynicism of some customers in overprotected items and the protection versus cost balance.

Packaging Easter eggs is essential to minimise breakage, and part of the unique Easter experience for kids. However, this is a time when the cynics loom large – they believe that the extortionate costs of kids' Easter eggs lies in overelaborate boxes. Be aware of anything you do that could be construed as such. However, it will probably depend on the target market you are selling to, for instance part of the appeal of some beauty products lies in the ostentatious packaging.

Packaging incurs costs in your business. We spoke in Chapter 1 about being wary of cutting costs that would result in a perception of a poorer quality offer. The same goes for packaging. I get livid in Tesco when their new cheaper and much thinner carrier bags mean I need to put less in each and so end up needing to carry more

Why packaging is important to get right

Silent Salesman
Displays an image you wish to stand for
Protection
Production/shelf space efficiency

to the car. Can you imagine if Tiffany, the jewellers, cut costs by ending the beautiful boxing, wrapping and bows on every purchase?

In terms of the functional protection role your packaging plays, you can go the other way and incur too many costs, which while guaranteeing undamaged goods can have some disadvantages. A soap detergent company used the strongest and thickest cardboard to box its powders. In cash and carries and stores the big boxes always ended up on the floor, with the competitors' weaker boxes piled on top. As a result customers could never see the strong-box brand (floor level is not a great level to attract shoppers) and if they did see it they couldn't manage to un-pile all the stock to get to the brand at the bottom. In a bid to revive sales the detergent company made the cardboard slightly thinner – still strong enough to protect the contents but not strong enough to support every other brand on display.

Packaging plays an extremely important role in the production process. Make sure any ideas you have for it are manageable with any manufacturing lines you use. The complexities you could add to the manufacturing process by going with intricate designs may outweigh the sales benefits you could gain. Hand packaging Royal Salute deluxe Scotch whisky in a velvet drawstring bag before boxing in luxurious embossed cartons is part of what the brand stands for and is a cost the price charged can cover. But would a Mr Kipling cherry slice be able to support the costs of sliding the plastic tray into the outer box by hand? Therefore don't ignore your production line when developing packaging.

The following consideration is also vital should your customers be the large supermarket chains or retailers. These chains have fairly sophisticated systems analysing the profit per space on shelf of any item. They also have detailed packages planning optimum shelf displays. So do not come up with really unusual fancy packaging

What makes great packaging?

Reflects target market
Protects contents
Functionally does what it should
Provides relevant information
Positions the product
Will have impact on shelf/display

before checking with these retailers that should they take it, it would fit on their shelves. They will look at the efficient use of the space it occupies versus the return they can make from selling it.

The section above should hopefully have planted some seeds of thought regarding packaging ideas you have and the importance of getting it right – these points are summarised in the table on p. 84. Before we move on to specifics of packaging development, I'll quickly summarise the characteristics of great packaging. It does of course vary market by market, but six key characteristics are outlined in the table above.

First, any packaging must always reflect the needs, tastes, behaviour, likes and dislikes of your target market.

Secondly, as mentioned earlier, it must protect but without cost being incurred in overprotection.

Thirdly, it must be functional and practical to use. We've seen shower gels that hang up in the shower, toilet cleaner that squirts up under the rim, oil cans where the pouring device doesn't get oil everywhere except in the oil tank. If your customer intends to display the products hanging from a rack on their wall, do you have holes in the packaging to hang the hook through? Ensure the packaging is practical to use and check where there is potential for differentiation.

Fourthly, it must carry the correct legal information. But it is up to you how much else you add by way of words and information. Is it already obvious or do you need more words to tell people what it is they are actually buying or what the product does? For some products only 5 per cent of customers read the label! Ensure your branding is strong and any information is relevant to the target market.

Fifthly, the packaging should of course reflect what the brand stands for – its positioning. Every single element must reflect the image and values of the brand. If you have a range of ideas for packaging, do a quick test with people around you. Show them the packaging options and rather than ask which they prefer, ask them which words they'd use to describe each. This is a much better way to check whether the packaging reflects the positioning you intend for your products.

Finally, consider the impact the packaging will have. You want it to stand out on shelf, while you want your carrier bags to stand out on the arm of the customer – it shouldn't be something they want to hide.

In order to come up with great packaging that lives up to the above characteristics, you should think about the effects of: colour, materials, shape/size, graphics and smell.

Colour can have very strong associations for people. In Japan people associate white with death, while in some South American countries that role goes to purple. Coffee manufacturers are well aware of these colour associations. Research has shown them that despite the same coffee being in each jar, people said the coffee that came from the brown labelled jar was strong, the red label was rich and the yellow label was weak. Because of the abundance of 'Special Offers' on show in many stores, some people associate the colours red and yellow as 'bargains' – not great therefore if you are a premium product. So check around as to whether there are strong colour associations in your market.

Some colour standards exist in markets that it may be wise to follow – the standard that tonic water comes with yellow labels, low fat or diet comes with white, bitter lemon comes with turquoise labels. Or you could challenge the standard in order to stand out. Red was the standard for Cola so Pepsi made their cans blue (admittedly it cost them an alleged £50 million). Walker's crisps challenged the standard that salt and vinegar packets were blue while cheese and onion were green by reversing the colours. It's now the standard understood by everyone under the age of 30 and still confuses others. Check whether there are colour standards you should follow or defy.

Which materials could you use in your packaging? For years watches came in leather, leather/look or plastic boxes, lined with leather or some substitute. Why do they have to come this way?

Storm watches use aluminium tins with coloured Perspex – perfect for the target market and the values of the brand. Origins is a range of environmentally friendly natural beauty products and cosmetics – to reinforce this positioning, they use natural, recycled packaging materials.

Physio Sport was a range of body products (shampoo, body wash, deodorant, talc) for the serious sportsperson, launched by Elida Fabergé. The products were made of materials easily manageable with wet hands in the shower or with sweaty hands.

The shape and size of any packaging is a consideration. Think how instantly recognisable the traditional Coca-Cola bottle is. Toblerone chocolate is another well-known brand, whose triangular packaging reflecting the Swiss Alps is impactful the world over. Wash & Go shampoo based its packaging design on a great customer insight – that customers who are in a rush in the shower do not have time to shake the shampoo bottle to get the product out. By designing a pack with a flat top the shampoo can be stored on its head so that the product comes out quickly even when the tiniest quantity remains in the bottle.

Most women's magazines are standard A4 size. The March 2001 launch of *Glamour* in A5 size was seen as a revelation – the first magazine to fit inside an average handbag, perfect for the target market, and impactful on the shelf.

Many great packaging examples are instantly recognisable even if the graphics are hidden or only partly visible. However, the graphics on your packaging in terms of both style and quantity still play a role. Go out to a supermarket and have a look at the Matchmakers and the After Eight packaging differences. Matchmakers is very fun looking while the After Eight graphics are much more formal. Think how the packaging of medicines make the products look.

Finally, ask whether smell has a role to play in your packaging. Many perfumed products deliberately allow the fragrance to permeate the packaging in order to stimulate the senses. L'Oréal launched a range of shampoo for children in fun-shaped bottles in bright colours, each bottle smelling of fruity flavours representing the shampoo fragrance. They cleverly built their packaging around another great insight – kids generally hate washing their hair but love the fun of toys at bath time and the smells of bubbles.

And that's packaging!

If you are trying to find a company to develop packaging for you then why not ask around in places you see great packaging – find out who developed it for them. And remember the six characteristics of great packaging, and use them to judge any ideas against.

The next section, merchandising and layout, is for those of you operating a shop. However, those of you interested in selling over the Internet (e-tailing) or through mail order, may find that there are many parallels.

Merchandising / layout

The first area we'll look at here is space – how you make the most of the available space to satisfy your target market. The quandary of making best use of your available sales space lies in the contradictions – look too cramped and busy and customers may be put off coming into the shop, look too empty and quiet and customers may feel uncomfortable entering. Packing every square foot of sales space with a product which could generate profit may make it difficult to shop when more than four customers are inside, while looking very minimalist may look unwelcoming and intimidating. Having a clear positioning will help here.

Go out to some competitors or other types of stores in your area and shop in them at different times of day. What is enjoyable and what is not?

One of the ladies' clothing retailers did some research into shopping habits. It indicated that the more women are jostled or even touched by other passing or browsing customers, the less time they spend in that store and the less likely they are to try on or purchase something.

Just as smell has a role to play in product packaging, so too is it important in store atmospherics – think of it as packaging your store. Our sense of smell is one of our most powerful and instinctive senses. Aromatherapy has long been recognised as having the ability to use fragrances to heal and lift spirits. While

I'm not suggesting you can use smell in your store to heal your customers, many businesses believe in the power of smell to trigger certain feelings and emotions in people. Hospitals and residential homes for the elderly are also using smell to portray a more positive impression of their businesses – even bright and cheery surroundings struggled to compete with the depressing smell of disinfectant and illness. Smell can make a hospital visit easier for both patient and visitor.

When selling your home you may have read the tips – have fresh flowers on display and coffee brewing in the kitchen. These smells trigger emotions of cleanliness and homeliness among potential buyers. Fresh ground coffee is frequently mentioned as a 'favourite' smell. One coffee company who sold fresh ground coffee in shopping centres was desperate to pump the smell of the coffee around the shopping centre. They looked into having the smell artificially created and pumped through the air vents. Unfortunately the smell was found to replicate stale tobacco rather than fresh coffee – wrong addiction.

Supermarkets use the smell of freshly baked bread to convey an image of welcoming and freshness. Many small convenience stores have benefited, too, from installing small bread ovens in their store, the aroma driving many impulse sales.

While you may not wish your store to smell of anything in particular, other than clean (that doesn't mean smelling of bleach), you may have no choice should your neighbours be fast-food restaurants or take-aways or smelly cheese shops. Hopefully you considered the smell implication on your stock before moving in.

Finally let's discuss how you could use layout to best sales effect. Unless your location is really well known and you offer something that people are prepared to make a special trip for (destination purchases), you probably rely on passing trade and your ability to drive impulse purchases. In addition to your shop window drawing people in, once inside, your layout can encourage impulse purchase. Rather than merchandise your stock by product type – sandwiches in one section, chocolate in another, crisps in another, fruit in another and soft drinks in another, you could merchandise by occasion – stock a range of all these items together in a snack section. Someone is more likely to buy a chocolate bar and some fruit and a drink in addition to their sandwich if it's close by and easy to find.

If you sell gents' shirts, you could display cufflinks at the till point as a last minute reminder and perhaps generate an impulse sale. If you sell ties, display them next to the shirts you suggest they complement.

I've been noticing recently how ladies' shoe shops draw in customers who are simply browsing. Rather than display the most common sizes (5–6) for browsers to try on, they have started to display very small sizes. This not only saves the sample shoe (which they will later sell) from being stretched and worn beyond all recognition, but it forces customers to ask an assistant for 'this one to try in a 5 please'. In drawing in the browser they hope to convert more store traffic into purchases. Of course, with this tactic comes the danger that whereas before at least people tried on the shoe and may have purchased it on impulse, now they may not even bother to ask for the shoe to try.

Within your store try to find out where your sales 'hotspots' are. In a supermarket they say that 'eye-level is buy-level'. The ends of aisles as you turn the corners are where they tend to put special offer items. Find out whether there are 'dead areas' in your store where people never tread and consider how to get them there.

If you are a service provider such as a hairdresser or insurance broker, try to have a layout where your reception desk is near the front of the store. Customers who are passing may be put off coming in if it's not clear where the desk is (especially if you have my eyesight and feel such an idiot wandering aimlessly).

Layout is about making it as easy as possible for someone to come in and buy from you. Stated like this I hope the parallels between a physical store layout and that of e-tailing sites or a mail-order brochure are clear. You may not have the benefit of smell (I'm sure technology will allow it soon enough), but you do have page layout, space you dedicate to each item, where you position each item in relation to others, how you sign people around, and in terms of your packaging you have a plethora of graphics, shapes and sizes open to you.

DISTRIBUTION

How will you reach your customers with your offer? Will you have a physical store? Will you deliver to them? How will you deliver? All of these are distribution issues.

In retailing they say there are three important things – location, location and location. Make sure the location for your outlet fits with your positioning – your image. Make sure that customers can find and reach you – what is parking going to be like, what else is nearby, will you get passing traffic? Therefore, as with most of marketing, your decisions are going to be driven by your target market. If I were a hairdresser targeting metropolitan trendy 20 and 30 somethings then I'd want to open the salon next to where these people lived, worked and socialised. I might look around for bars, cafés and shops also targeting these customers.

Say you run a small furniture store. What is your delivery plan? Will you buy or rent a van specifically for your business in order to make deliveries to customers? Who will drive the van to make those deliveries if not you? What will you do with the shop if you are out making deliveries because the driver didn't turn up or you can't afford one? Maybe you'll contract out the delivery to a local company who specialises in these logistics. Make sure you are totally clear about the way this company will charge you. They may go by weight of item, space in the truck the item occupies, a sliding fixed scale based on quantity of items or a flat fee. What about insurance? Find out up-front so that there are no surprises you may need to pass on to the customer.

Additionally, think carefully about one of the biggest things you are in danger of losing (after the goods) should you use a contract delivery company – control. He gives priority to another company's customer, he is rude to the customer and he won't help carry the item up stairs into the customer's house. You have no right to the excuse that he doesn't really work for you. The customer does not care. All they want is their furniture – everything about that furniture from the quality of the materials from which it is constructed to the way it is carried into the home will be attributed to your small furniture shop.

Now let's talk more about delivery policy from the customer's point of view – whether you sell through a mail-order catalogue, over the Internet or from a warehouse direct to your customers. I'm thinking here of goods that are too large to fit through the average letterbox. I buy only very occasionally from mail-order catalogues, because I live in a household where we work and are not at home all day. Despite what the seller says, sometimes I just can't land my delivery on a friendly neighbour who'll sign for it on my behalf, and to be honest, how many people are lucky enough to know their neighbours that well? I cannot bear the hassle of trying to arrange a convenient delivery time. 'I'll be at home on Tuesday', 'No, I'm sorry we don't deliver to your area on Tuesdays, only Mondays or Fridays'. 'If you could deliver on Friday before 12 noon I could be at home to sign for it.' 'No, I'm sorry, we cannot give you a delivery time as specific as that.' And what happens should you be lucky enough to have been able to be at home to receive your goods, only to find that they are the wrong colour, wrong size, pieces are missing out of your flat pack or are the totally wrong items? 'You need to pack it back up in the box as it was when you received it, and we will be able to collect it on Monday or Friday.' 'No, I'm sorry we can't give you a time.'

McCord is a mail-order company (part of the huge GUS catalogue empire) who specialise in furniture, furnishings and accessories for every room in the home. I had an experience with McCord recently when trying to order bookcases, which has confirmed all my fears about mail-order shopping. Goods ordered, fine. Delivery time: 'I'm sorry I can't tell you that as the items do not come from our warehouse, they are large and so will come direct from the supplier. When the goods are ready the supplier, who uses a courier delivery company, will have the courier call you to arrange a delivery time.' 'I will not be at home to receive that call, so could they call me at work?' 'Sure, no problem, I'll tell them.' Two weeks later still no phone call. So I have to call McCord who promise to call the supplier, who say they are ready and the delivery company should have called. I'm given the number for the delivery company. 'Oh we tried to deliver those last week but there was no answer.' 'Yes, that'll be because I work! I asked for a phone call so I could arrange a convenient time with you.' 'That's McCord for you, we were never told that.' 'Well can I rearrange a time now?' 'OK what about tomorrow?' 'No, I'm sorry that's too short notice for me to rearrange tomorrow's meetings and stay at home. Can you do next Wednesday?' 'OK that's fine. The bookcases will be with you between 1 and 9 pm. No we can't be any more specific than that.' Well eventually the goods arrived and the flat pack building commenced. And do you know what I discovered after all this? – only two of the three bookcases had been delivered. And so began the repeat process of trying to get my third item. Of course McCord got full payment weeks ago! And did I get one apology? On not one of the many occasions I spoke with McCord did one person say sorry.

So your brochure/mail-order catalogue can look great, the prices can be fine and the range and style of the products on offer ideal. But if you fail to get the items to your customers painlessly and in reasonable time, everything else is useless – how long will it be before I give McCord a second chance? As a small company, look to see where competitors (even large ones) are getting it wrong in areas such as their delivery policy. Take advantage of this and put it right. Find out the weaknesses of competitors in the market and see whether it provides an opportunity for you.

Another example: Ocean is a mail-order catalogue full of furniture, garden, bedroom, lighting and kitchenware: 'Style for the modern home' is how they describe their goods. I saw the catalogue lying somewhere and would never have looked based on my McCord experience, were it not for three words on the front cover – 'NEW! Evening Deliveries'. So I took a look. 'For only £2 extra you can have an evening delivery, within 48 hours (delivered between 5 pm and 9 pm).' For the convenience of narrowing the time I have to wait at home, and no need to wait weeks for it to come, I would be happy to pay £2 extra. When you read the pricing chapter you will see how this relates to one of the rules on pricing – charge for what you know customers place value on.

Tesco normally use white vans, branded with the Tesco name to make home deliveries. They have a group of customers – the wealthy class conscious – who are embarrassed to be seen buying from the supermarket. Many are switching from Harrods and

Fortnums, but don't want the neighbours to know. Therefore, instead of a white van driven by a man in a supermarket uniform, the delivery is made in a four-wheel drive by a man in a suit. The vehicles have tinted windows and carry only tiny Tesco badges. Distribution to meet the customers' needs.

Another example of a great integrated and consistent offer based on the target market is that of Pharmacy Plus. They are a small chain of, just as it says, pharmacies – but unlike other high street competitors sell no consumer products such as shampoos, baby products or beauty products. They are adamant that their business is medicine – a very clear positioning. They target people who need medical advice for minor conditions but who don't want to, or can't wait for a doctor's appointment. They have highly trained pharmacists and staff in all branches who are able to help with the diagnosis and treatment of minor problems. To make people more comfortable discussing their problems they have consulting rooms where you can speak in private with the pharmacist – rather than have Doris next in the queue for her verruca cream hearing your personal worries. Such rooms project the right image for the stores – after all, how can you solve problems when your customers are too embarrassed to share all of them with you? They also have a prescription home delivery service for those unable to get to the store to collect their doctor-provided prescription. This satisfies the needs of the home bound or the 'too busies'.

Perhaps you make sandwiches, baguettes and cakes to sell with fruit, crisps and drinks as snacks. What are your distribution plans? Will you have a shop where you prepare and sell? Will you open all day or just at lunchtime? Will you offer a delivery service to local offices and businesses? Will you go around offices mid-morning and mid-afternoon selling from your basket/van? How else and where else can you get to your target customers? Will local hospitals allow you to sell your wares to visitors? Do the railway or bus station used by local commuters offer potential to sell? Marks & Spencer have a pretty good reputation for their sandwiches and realise that many potential sales are lost, as customers can't get to their stores. So they considered their distribution options. If the customer can't get to them, they could get to the customer. As a result, in early 2001 M&S were in the process of signing an agreement with W H Smith based in railway stations to stock M&S sandwiches. I would imagine the deal is a pretty expensive one, with either an upfront sum, or a percentage of takings being passed on to W H Smith. This reinforces further the need to be different from the competition. Big players are out there looking to capture business in areas that traditionally would have been the grounds of smaller businesses. If you wanted your sandwiches stocked at a railway station, what could you offer W H Smith that they couldn't get from M&S – certainly not a cash incentive.

If you want to stay ahead of the game with your distribution plans and route to market, be creative in your choice of distribution. Keep your target customer in your mind and think about them 24 hours a day. Throughout a day in the life of a typical customer, where are all the places you could reach them with your product or service? A book publisher producing books on gardening would be mad to ignore selling in garden centres, while an aerobics-wear business could consider selling direct to customer in the local gym or health club.

Are there any other products or services which complement yours? Would offering your product or service alongside another add to the experience and add to the value perceived in the offer? Do not ignore approaching existing businesses and assessing the potential to join forces with them. If you are a manicurist, perhaps a local hairdressing salon would allow you to work out of their salon offering your service to their customers. It would be much more cost effective and less risky in the early days than paying a huge property overhead on your own. Just make sure you have a contract that details how to end the arrangement should your business take off so much that you need to move to larger premises.

Before we move on to look at the other elements of the marketing mix which go to form part of your offer and experience, do not forget that it cannot remain static. You have got to change to keep up with the changing market and changing tastes over the life of your offer. What is desirable as an experience last year may not be so attractive next year – don't get complacent.

SUMMARY CHECKLIST

■ Your offer is the totality of everything you do

■ You develop your total offer using the elements of the marketing mix: product or service core, pricing, communication, distribution and people/customer service

■ It is vitally important that all elements of the mix are consistent with each other

■ You develop your marketing mix based on the target customer needs, the competition and what you want to stand for as a product/business

■ Some things in your mix you may offer for all customers, while others you offer specifically for specific target customers within your target market – but beware expensive proliferation and remember the 80 : 20 rule

■ Positioning your offer means knowing what you want to stand for in the mind of your target customers compared to the competition. It means clarifying the functional and emotional benefits customers will obtain

■ Get your product or service core right or the rest of the marketing mix is pointless

■ Packaging protects and acts as a Silent Salesman for your products. Make sure your packaging reflects customer needs, offers relevant and legal information, functions properly, protects the contents, positions the contents and has impact

■ Make the most of your selling space by using merchandising and layout to encourage purchase

■ You need to get your product or service to the customer, and the distribution element of the mix means deciding how best to do this.

5
How to Set Prices

There's no going back from the first price you set.
Andy F. Bryce

THE CHAPTER AT A GLANCE

Pricing is the only element of your marketing mix concerned with bringing in money – the communication, product development, distribution, websites, and customer services parts of your marketing mix are all costs to your business, invested in the hope of incentivising purchase. So price is important.

Everything else in your mix might be great, but if a customer doesn't think your product or service is worth the price then the potential sale is lost. Along with the actual or perceived quality, price allows a customer to put a value on something. A Lada for £10 000 is not worth it, but a Ford Focus may be.

Understanding the value customers place on your products and services is key to great pricing strategy – and is known as value-based pricing. Once we have looked at the importance of getting your pricing right and the influences on your pricing, this chapter looks at value based pricing as one strategy you could adopt.

THE IMPORTANCE OF
GETTING YOUR PRICING RIGHT

Get the price wrong and you could undermine everything you have worked hard to get in place. It is very easy to get your pricing wrong – and extremely dangerous. If the price is too high, there is no demand. Once people think you stand for overpriced products, it's difficult to change their perception and get them to look again once your prices are reduced a bit. If you are seen to be reducing prices, customers might think you're in trouble, you're not doing well, the quality is not that good or, worse, they might delay purchase thinking your prices are going to come down even further.

However, it is much easier to reduce prices that are too high than it is to increase those that are too low. If you price too low, can you cover your costs? What if your suppliers were to put up their prices – could you still cover your costs? If you price too low, it may make people think your goods are of poor quality. Price too low and you could end up out of pocket as people would have been prepared to pay more – sacrificing profits after all you've done so far!

In general, most new and small businesses charge too little for their goods and especially their services. The temptation is to think that you'd rather have a sale than no sale, even if it means not breaking even. (Breaking even means the point at which you are selling enough to just cover your overheads, where profit = zero.)

I spoke to many small businesses when writing this book and at least two of them told me that they had priced far too low in the beginning, so keen were they to get business, and they're still paying for it now.

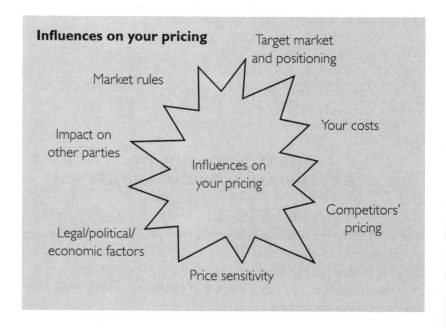

Influences on your pricing

Target market and positioning

Market rules

Impact on other parties

Influences on your pricing

Your costs

Competitors' pricing

Legal/political/ economic factors

Price sensitivity

To help get your pricing right there are some key influences you should consider. These are shown below.

INFLUENCES ON YOUR PRICING

Let's look at the seven influences shown in the diagram, as those are the key factors to consider in any attempt at setting prices.

Target market and positioning

If your target market is clear, pricing becomes slightly easier. Defining the customers you are hoping to satisfy comes after understanding their needs and wants, which hopefully has thrown some light on what they might be willing to pay. By having a clear positioning – knowing what you want to stand for – you are likely to find it easier to reach a price that is consistent with the rest of your marketing mix. Pricing a Jaguar, with its clear premium luxury positioning, is much easier than pricing a Rover for example, where positioning is not quite so clear. Häagen-Dazs ice cream when launched (very clearly as a premium ice cream) ensured that their pricing strategy was in line with their high-quality product, image and intended positioning – to have priced cheaply would have contradicted everything in their marketing mix and probably have made consumers question the quality of the product itself. In its early days Häagen-Dazs ensured that pricing levels were kept premium – they did not price discount in supermarkets or stores.

An agency recently launched for fashion stylists and photographers deliberately priced themselves at the top end of the market. This was to maintain the prestige of the people on their books, who work for fashionable glossy magazines such as *Vogue*.

The agency owners understood that in the fashion industry there is a certain amount of snobbery – clients expect higher prices. If they set lower prices, clients would perceive them as a less prestigious agency. However, bear in mind that customers are generally becoming much more value-savvy.

Your costs

Obvious statement coming up – you will only make a profit if your revenue exceeds your costs. Ask yourself how much you must charge as a minimum in order to cover your basic running costs; all of your basic running costs, both fixed and variable. If a customer abroad wants to buy your products, you must build these export costs into your equation. Look at the different levels of profit you could make selling at different prices with your current cost structure. Some businesses have a high percentage of their total costs as fixed costs – costs the business incurs whether they sell or not. For example a hotel or B & B is high fixed cost – they incur the cost of keeping the property open and staffed whether they have 10 per cent occupancy or 100 per cent. When times are hard businesses like this cut prices in order to improve occupancy and cover their fixed costs of business. So long as the price they charge covers the additional variable costs of the lighting in the room, any meal the guests have, any drinks in the bar and any other costs incurred in that extra guest staying then they are no worse off. Just beware such pricing does not stop people ever paying full price for your hotel room.

Your competitors

It is not really possible to set prices without knowing those of your competitors, both direct and indirect. If I were an airline setting prices for flights to Paris from London, I'd want to know not only the prices of other airlines (my direct competitors), but also the ferry companies, Eurotunnel and Eurostar as indirect competitors. Ask yourself if you offer any advantages over the competition, any differentiation, which would allow you to price slightly higher. If you were to raise your prices in the market while your competitors did not, how would you justify it? Customers might not care that it's because your costs have gone up – they may go to a competitor if their products or services are perceived as identical to yours. I am not saying you must be cheaper than the competition – if all else is identical in the offer, including the seller and how much he is liked, then, yes, maybe the cheapest of the options will win. But very rarely is all else identical. There may be something (however minute in the cost incurred by you) that you can do or offer, or be perceived as having in your total offer, that makes the customer prepared to pay a little more than your competitors are charging. A fascinating example, very relevant today, is that of the price of Internet access. Many customers signed up with Screaming on the basis of how cheap access and calls were. However, many are unhappy with the standard of service. In addition to proving difficult to connect at peak times, access has been unreliable and technical support poor. One customer said he left his phone on automatic redial for four hours trying to get through to the helpline. That customer has since switched to Freeserve. He knows it is more expensive per month for access, but he believes it is worth the extra money.

So check out what the competition is charging. Without being too sneaky, you could get friends to pose as customers and ask for quotes. If you are leaving an employer to set up on your own as a competitor, you have the advantage of knowing what the average charging rates are.

Price sensitivity

When setting a price for the first time or when considering making changes to any price, you must bear in mind the price sensitivity of your goods among your target customers. This will be linked to the prices of your competitors. If you were to raise your price, how much would volume fall? What would happen to volume if you were to drop the price? Would price changes affect volume? Strongly branded products tend to be less price sensitive than those that have no strong differentiation – if I want Kellogg's Special K, I'm not that sensitive to a 10p per box price increase, whereas if I bought Tesco own wheat flakes I may notice a 10p price increase and deem it less acceptable. Ask if your offer is differentiated enough to be unprice sensitive. When the duty on cigarettes and alcohol increases and results in price increases across the board, people who smoke or drink may not cut their consumption. The markets are not price sensitive in that way. However, if you were to increase the price of your cigarettes in isolation to the market, with no apparent differentiation or customer loyalty, pricing would be very sensitive and volume may suffer as customers switch brand. Some products or services are price sensitive due to timing or seasonality – at Disneyland Paris I may need to cut my price in winter to encourage visitors, but certainly wouldn't need to in summer. My sensitivity to the price of photocopier paper is low if the paper only accounts for a tiny percentage of the running costs of my business, but high if my business is photocopying. Customers are more sensitive to the prices of necessities than they are non-essentials and more price sensitive to items they buy frequently than to occasional purchases – so do you know where you stand?

Legal / economic / political factors

If the government changes the levels of VAT or duty on your products you should be planning the effects on your pricing. The slight consolation is that the changes will affect you *and* your competitors – but by how much? If you rely on exports for the bulk of your business, have you considered the effect on your pricing in that market should the local importing country change the import duty levied on foreign purchases?

In October 2000 Ford Motors announced (following similar decisions by other car manufacturers) a reduction to the list prices of their models. It is fair to say that this strategy didn't follow months of detailed analysis by Ian McAllister the MD of Ford UK, but as a result of continued political pressure and consumers sourcing from cheaper European and Internet dealers. They have decided to end all 'promotional incentives' such as cash back, free insurance and go instead for straightforward price cuts. (My question is how long it will be before the customer gets cheaper list prices *and* the promotional incentives again – once the car pricing has stabilised at a lower level what do they have to compete with if the brand is not strong enough?)

Impact on other parties

If you set your prices at a much higher level than your competitors, make sure your salesforce understand the reasons why. If they cannot justify the premium to customers, they may lose faith in what they have to sell.

If you sell your products to distributors, wholesalers or retailers who sell on to the end customer, please make sure you consider them in the price equation. Build in any margin they require. Carefully plan the pricing incentives you offer these customers – there's always the risk of upsetting someone who thinks another customer got a better deal. Should you need to cut prices how accepting will the customer be of reduced profit they stand to make in selling on to the end customer? If you propose to increase prices, will they demand more margin to help sell out the product to the end customer?

Market rules

Are there any standards or rules when it comes to pricing in your market? Does a painter charge per day or per job? Does your health club charge per visit or per month? Do you charge a different rate for peak and off-peak hours? Do you charge per page, per day or per contract for Internet page design?

Are you going to go with the standards your competitors follow or will you challenge these standards and set your own pricing guidelines? If you decide to challenge the rules then make sure it is blatantly clear to the customers what they should expect to pay.

In the market offering Internet access, one of the 'rules' seemed to be that you needed to offer 'free' access. However, if you were to examine the offers of competitors very closely then in actual fact, very few of the services were actually 'free'. In summer 2000 the *Sunday Times* featured an article showing that there were numerous conditions which customers had to fulfil in order to qualify for 'free' access. Customers had to pay monthly registration fees, spend minimum monthly amounts on phone calls, change their telephone service supplier, pay for special adaptors, only receive free access in off-peak hours – the conditions went on. Imagine as a customer how difficult it is to compare prices in this market. The service is promoted as 'free', but it is not at all.

Imagine as a customer how difficult it is to compare prices in this market. In his brilliant book designed to mock the political shortcomings of large organisations and people in them, *The Dilbert Principle*,[1] Scott Adams jokes about companies playing 'Confusopoly' – the deliberate game of trying to make your pricing as confusing as possible to every customer so that they find it hard to know if you are good value or not. If you find yourself in a market where the rules of the pricing structure say you need to be a certain way 'free' (as in the Internet service providers) make it clear to customers exactly how much your service or goods really cost. They will appreciate the honesty – look at Virgin as an example of how to enter the mobile phone market and cut through the confusing tariff structures. Also, as another way of differentiating, take time to shout about everything else that you do that might justify why you are slightly more expensive – technical support, 24-hour helpline, guaranteed response and quote within 24 hours, cost and availability of follow-up help or parts.

So what approach to pricing will you take, having considered all these factors – what will be your pricing strategy?

PRICING STRATEGIES

I am going to briefly mention three different approaches to pricing you could adopt: cost-plus, going rate and value-based.

Cost-plus pricing

This takes your costs involved per sale, adds a margin you think is acceptable in your market, and comes up with a sales price. While simple to understand it is quite hard to allocate some costs (what percentage of heating costs of your office will you allocate to the costs of your different graphic design packages?). Cost-plus pricing alone ignores what the competition are charging or what the customers are prepared to pay. In few markets do customers try to calculate the costs that went into production and decide whether the mark-up is acceptable or not. Some element of your pricing may be partly cost based, but you shouldn't use it as the sole strategy, independent of competitor and customer understanding. A city centre hairdresser may charge more for a haircut than a rural salon – but the customer does not happily pay the higher price because of location, but probably because of the image that comes with the location. A senior partner in a law firm may charge more than a junior partner. The client does not happily pay more because it costs the law firm more to employ a senior partner, but because the client gets the benefit of his experience and so a better service.

Going rate pricing

Going rate pricing involves a strong understanding of the com-petitive market independent of your costs. If a junior hairdresser charges an average of £20 for women's cut and blow drying and £12 for gents', you'd price in line with this going rate. If local builders charge £120 per day labour plus materials then you may go with this price too. Please make sure though that you are not undercharging. The going rate is a great benchmark if your product or service is identical to that of the competitors. But if you have based your offer on an understanding of a target market and insight into their needs and developed a differentiated offer for them, is there scope to charge a slight premium? £100 might be the daily rate for a standard painter and decorator, but if I could find one who'd give colour scheme suggestions and suggest coordinated décor to complement the effect then I know he'd be worth more than £100. Knowing worth to a customer leads us on to value-based pricing.

Value-based pricing

This involves determining just how much you are worth to the customer, how much he or she values what you have to offer, and pricing accordingly. If you have no concept of how much you are worth to a customer, you risk over- or underpricing. Try to find out what your customers value about your product, or place value on in the market in which you compete. If you can offer attributes which they value, they will be less price sensitive. A Massey Ferguson tractor may be priced at £5000 more than another competitor. But farmers may place value on the fact that it costs less to service, parts are cheaper when out of warranty, the warranty itself is five years rather than three years and the resale value is higher. A paper cup of tepid coffee costing 50p may be value at a roadside van on a wet day, whereas I may be quite happy to pay £2 for a cappuccino in a coffee bar smelling of fresh ground coffee and offering the day's newspapers. I might see £1 as outrageous for a bar of soap, but great value for a bar of soap formulated for sensitive skin.

For years Coca-Cola have been great exponents of value-based pricing. Next time you go into a supermarket have a look at the difference in price per litre of a two-litre bottle and a can straight from the refrigerator and ready to drink. I think it's become pretty much accepted now in the market that to buy in larger sizes is more cost effective, so cans were always more expensive per litre than two-litre bottles. But Coca-Cola have realised that on a hot, sunny day people really value being able to buy a can of Coke they can drink to quench their thirst there and then – in such a season (or the odd day in the UK!). Coke know the value on the ready-chilled can is really high and people are less price sensitive, so they can price a bit higher.

The danger of this strategy, of course, is being seen as ripping off the consumer – but remember consumers are not stupid, they really would vote with their feet if they were so outraged. As indeed they do in some outlets which take this inflated charging a bit too far – ice cream vans by the beach on that one hot week of summer every year, charging over 200 per cent more than shops for a chilled can, because of 'value' they are offering to people who don't want to walk far to the nearest shop. There is a fine line.

I heard an interesting story about tests around value-based pricing which Coca-Cola were running, in Asia I think it was, in their vending machines. Each vending machine had an in-built thermometer and a device which automatically changed the price per drink as the temperature changed – people value an immediate cold drink more in hotter temperatures so were prepared to pay a bit more.

Madan Singh is an engineering professor who believed he had a great product for determining prices to charge, but he failed to interest customers until he started charging steeply for it. He had developed a theory to show how the pricing of products could have an impact on sales. He approached companies such as BP, Midland Bank and NatWest and had no trouble getting an audience. The companies were excited about his product and discussions, but it never went any further than that. His offers of free trials never came to anything – he couldn't find a way to close the deal. After 20 lunches and not getting anywhere he drew the conclusion that what he was offering was not attractive because he had not put a value on it – he was selling his services too cheaply. Rather than looking to the value of what he was offering customers he was comparing it to his salary. A revision of prices to a much higher level allowed him to bill £1 million over the first five years. At the start of 2000 the company was floated on the Stock Exchange, valued at £163 million.

SOME FINAL TIPS

Set high prices if you don't want the work

Pricing always seems to be spoken about in a way that relates to getting people to buy from you – what is the best price to encourage people to buy? Well, when the occasion demands, it can also be quite helpful to think about it the other way round: what price will encourage people not to buy? I know it sounds bizarre but there may genuinely be occasions when you'd rather not sell to someone – a customer who you know is really hard to deal with and who you'd rather not supply; where stock is a problem and you'd like to prioritise deliveries to only your top clients; a client who you'd really rather not sell to for fear of damaging your image and reputation; or you just don't want to do the work. Rather than say you don't want the work, it's probably better to let the customer choose not to buy from you – set your prices too high. I was recently quoted an amazing price by someone to fit a new stair banister – he didn't want the work so priced himself out of the market, and it worked.

Imagine you are the guy making the baby-feeding products mentioned in Chapter 1 – the last thing you want is for them to be sold heavily discounted only on the basis of price, as it would totally remove all the value built into the perception of the premium quality of the products. To control the outlets you sell through you could make your pricing so unattractive that it discourages some of them. Just make sure that those outlets can't buy elsewhere at low rates and so upset the stability of pricing in the market.

Never overpromise and underdeliver

An example of a businesses saying the price is X and then it turns out to be quite a bit higher is in the very competitive car-hire industry. Stelios Haji-Ioannou, is the people's champion, the head of the Easy-Group empire; he offers customers his wares at prices that prove how much they have been ripped off by the big, established companies in the market. He provides Internet access through his high street shops (EasyEverything) at £1 per hour, no frills flights (EasyJet) to destinations at no frills prices, and now EasyRentacar. This venture was set up when he spotted the potential to cut through the disguised pricing of car rental. He knew that it irritated customers to see adverts quoting £29 to rent a car for the day, only to try to make a booking and discover that by the time mandatory and optional taxes, insurances, mileage rates and extra driver fees were added in, it took the cost to almost double this rate. So there you have it: a Mercedes A-class for £9 per day. Impressive at £13.55 per day less than the next cheapest and £56 cheaper than the most expensive – if the sales pitch were true, this simple pricing approach had the potential to totally change the economics and rules of the industry.

But if you look closer then in fact this offer of clarity of pricing and cheap pricing may be misleading. Bookable only via the Internet, customers will find that when they sign on, every booking is subject to a £5 preparation fee (yes, it is in the advertising, but in very small letters). This is charged for a maintenance check and cleaning the car (OK so it is admirable that he does this on every car, but as customers have no choice about it being done or not then the price is *never* going to be £9). Then if customers travel further than 75 miles they will find the bill increases by 20p for every additional mile. In the industry, the average car is rented for a weekend and the average distance travelled is 500 miles. At this mileage an EasyRentacar would cost £137, almost £15 more than even its most expensive rival, and double the cost of its cheapest. The £9 per day rate (before preparation) applies to a rental where the car is picked up in the morning and returned the same evening. Competitors' rates run on a morning to following morning basis. To replicate rivals EasyRentacar will charge £16.50 for full 24-hour rental (so again it is not £9 per day as the consumer perceives a day to mean in the language of car rental). So all included (and I haven't taken time to mention the larger excess for which you will be liable under EasyRentacar) it is good value if you do not intend to drive any further than around 100 miles and you can guarantee you will bring the Mercedes A-class back without a scratch on it. Oh, and did I mention that while driving your lovely Mercedes A-class then you have to suffer the indignity of driving it around (not too far remember!) complete with orange EasyRentacar logo on each side? Great for EasyRentacar advertising, less good for you if you have just picked up the car at the airport and need to arrive at a potential client's office in style.

In 2000, the *Sunday Times* researched the car-hire market comparing the daily car rental rates for Easyrentacar, Avis, Hertz, Europecar, Sixt, Budget, Kenning, Alamo and National. They compared the daily price for car hire when driving between 100 and 500 miles. If driving 100 miles, Easyrentacar is your cheapest option, at a cost of £21.50, although Avis is not far behind at £22.55. The most expensive was Alamo at £65.55. However, when driving 500 miles Easyrentacar was by far the most expensive option at a cost of £101.50. Avis still only cost £22.55 and the closest price to Easyrentacar was Alamo, still at their 100 mile rate of £65.55.

Now I am not saying that a potential customer will sit down and compare prices to this degree, but how do you think they feel when someone does it for them and highlights how misleading your adverts and promises have been?

So my tip here is: yes, go ahead, challenge the rules, make it easier and simpler for the customer to see why your offer is better value and does not attempt to hide anything. But make sure it does just that – be up-front and honest about all the things you will charge for, there should be no surprises for the customer. If you are not sure what the final price will be it is better to overestimate in the initial stages and then undercharge on delivery.

Give notice of price increases

Especially if you are selling to other businesses, give notice of any forthcoming price increases in writing, with at least three months' notice, explaining why – it's only common courtesy.

SUMMARY CHECKLIST

- Set your price too low and it's hard to put it up
- Your target market, desired positioning, your costs, external factors, market rules, competitors' pricing, price sensitivity in your market and the projected impact on your salesforce and distributors must be considered when setting prices
- Cost plus pricing may undervalue your offer
- Going rate pricing is fine if you have no differentiation
- Value-based pricing puts customer requirements at the heart of your pricing
- Set prices high if you don't really want the work, but be sure you won't need it in the future
- Never promise one price and fail to deliver through adding on extras
- Inform people of any price increases.

6

Communication Plans

How to tell customers about you and your offer

I know that half my advertising is
wasted, but I don't know which half.
John Wanamaker

THE CHAPTER AT A GLANCE

'If you build it they will come' may work in Hollywood for Kevin Costner and his baseball field. You may have a fantastic understanding of your target market with real insight into their needs and wants, developed a fantastic product or service for them, detailed your pricing plans, have distribution in place and an excellent customer service policy. But if no one knows that you exist, or where you are and what you have to offer then you're never going to sell anything. How are you going to get people to use your baseball field? The communication part of your marketing mix is vital to the success of your offer.

This chapter looks at how to make the most of your communication tactics using the budget you have (or maybe don't have). Having identified the various communication methods you could use, it looks at what makes great communication and what drives great and effective communication – your target audience and your objectives. It then looks into specific guidelines for using the alternative methods and finally the need to evaluate your activity.

METHODS OF COMMUNICATING

Depending on the business you are and the types of customers you have then the communication methods open to you are vast: advertising, direct mail, sponsorship, exhibitions, open days, sales promotion offers, public relations, personal word of mouth and personal selling. The chapter will go on to look in detail at the main ones.

The difficulty lies not in deciding whether to communicate, but how to communicate; which methods you should use. The drivers of this will probably be: your budget, the specific target audience and your objectives.

Whichever methods you choose you want them to be as effective as possible. If you use advertising, you don't want half of it to be wasted. So, before we look at target audience and objectives in detail, it is worth considering what we mean by great and effective communication.

THE CHARACTERISTICS
OF GREAT COMMUNICATION

Whether it is advertising or brochures, press releases or direct mail letters, exhibition stands or demonstrations, you want them all to be as great as possible.

People will tell you that it has got cheaper and cheaper to reach customers with messages, but in fact it has got more expensive. Why? Information and communication overload. There is only so much time people will give to communications – they filter many out. Our brains haven't got bigger, but the number of messages trying to get through is rising. So the cost of getting the attention of customers among all the other thousands of communications is actually rising. Therefore the only way to ensure your messages reach your customers is to make sure they have the five characteristics of:

1. Relevance – make sure the message and the way you deliver it is relevant to the target audience and to the type of product or service you are offering

2. Impact – any communication should stand out and grab attention
3. Memorability – ensure your product or service will be remembered
4. Consistency – the communication must be consistent with your positioning, the image of your product or service and with the rest of the marketing mix, but also with other communication messages
5. Simplicity – it should contain simple and clear messages.

If a marketing message is not relevant to a customer, it has been a waste of your money and the customer's time. Relevant messages provide added value to the customer and hopefully get good response rates for you. In being relevant you are on the way to cutting through the clutter, standing out, having impact and being remembered. You are more likely to have impact if your piece of communication, at the time it is seen, heard, opened or smelt, has relevance to the customer.

Think about some examples: the government messages for safe driving will be most relevant if placed anywhere cars are driving or where the effects of accidents are in the forefront of the mind. So toilets in motorway service stations (tiredness from long journeys makes driving safety relevant), car park tickets, leaflets or posters around schools would all be great places to advertise or communicate.

What about your window cleaning service – what would be relevant ways to communicate? How about leaflets, placed face down, on car windscreens outside houses on residential streets? Having to read the text through a more than likely dirty windscreen may prompt some people to think about how dirty their house windows are. Even more relevant would be to place your leaflets through letterboxes or on cars on a sunny day, just after a week or so of dreadful weather – guaranteed that windows, everyone's, will be in need of cleaning.

If you are a dentist, when may your services be really relevant? What about brides-to-be preparing for their big day? Having white teeth for all the photos is a big worry. So perhaps you could think about taking stands at local wedding fairs, or looking in your local newspaper for engagement announcements.

For teenage products and services such as music, videos, hairstyling and fashion, make sure your timing is relevant. Focus on communicating to your target market just before the weekend as they are getting ready to go out and spend their pocket money.

I particularly liked the Tetley's Bitter communication in 1998/9. They were aiming to become a national bitter brand and position themselves as 'Ruggedly Smooth'. As a sponsor of Rugby Union they focused all their activity on rugby: pub promotions, promotions and offers on cans bought in supermarkets and off-licences, radio and press advertising, some PR competitions in sports magazines, 'Kick for £1m' promotions, direct mail to rugby clubs, poster adverts on all South West Trains (the lines servicing routes to Twickenham) and my personal favourite: mini posters in gents toilets of over 200 Tetley's pubs throughout England. The impact came from the words 'Beware – Loose Balls'. An expensive and complicated communication programme, yes, but the learning is there for you whatever your budget – the more relevant to the target market and situation the target market might be in when faced with the message, the more likely you will have impact.

The problem is that everyone will be trying to do the same thing and as a result of searching for relevance, we are back to even more clutter to stand out from, and the danger of heightening customer annoyance at the plethora of messages received. So if the competition is focusing hard on where messages will be relevant, don't rule out using totally surprising places, times or messages.

The Wonderbra poster campaign certainly had *impact* and that alone made it one of the most *memorable* pieces of communication. It was, of course, also relevant to the target audience – women who could get a boost to their cleavage physically and a boost to their confidence emotionally. It was an extremely *simple and clear* message, and the style was used consistently and became instantly recognisable as Wonderbra ads and the Wonderbra girl. So while you probably don't plan to spend a few hundred thousand on a poster campaign, you must ensure that anything you plan is going to have impact – otherwise it will be ignored, thrown in the bin or flicked over.

Having a *clear and simple* message sounds the easiest to achieve, but in fact it is probably one of the areas where most communication lets itself down. The temptation is to use the communication opportunity to say everything for fear of leaving out the one vital piece of information people may need to know. In trying to do this you probably forget the need to be relevant to specific individuals and you certainly lose impact or memorability. One piece of communication cannot do everything for you – choose carefully what you want each to achieve otherwise you risk being cluttered and confusing. By using a range of methods each saying a clear and simple message, you will get your full information across much more effectively. M&S created a great piece of simple communication for their Footglove range. This was a small four-page leaflet that came inside my M&S chargecard bill. Rather than try to say everything about the shoe on the front page – the quality of the leather, the style of the shoes, the value in the price, the softness of the material, the comfort for the wearer, they focused on one key benefit based on customer insight: 'M&S Footglove shoes – the shoes your feet have been aching for.' Inside the leaflet they spoke of other benefits.

A piece of communication I personally believe not to be great is the monthly mailing from the *Sunday Times* Wine Club. It is not simple at all, there are far too many different leaflets and sheets and pages inside each envelop. It is not memorable, and while every month it is consistent with the look of the previous month I really don't think it does justice to the values and image of the *Sunday Times*. I don't even bother reading it all anymore – I go to the new wines page and bin the rest. What a waste of money for the *Sunday Times*.

In trying to decide which method of communication to use and to make whichever method you choose as effective as possible, it is important to know exactly what you want to say, to whom and why.

WHO IS YOUR SPECIFIC TARGET AUDIENCE?

Of course any communication is going to be based on your target market – that message has been clear throughout the book so far.

However, when it comes down to the detail of who exactly you are aiming your advert or direct mail or press articles at, then you probably need to be much more specific. If you were Next and you wanted to promote your mail-order Home Furnishings catalogue, are you going to focus on current Next customers or all shoppers, are you going to focus on people who are current mail-order shoppers or any shopper, are you going to focus on people who have bought from the Home Furnishing catalogue already or on Next shoppers who have not? It's a really important area to get right, because your decision will determine the type of message you use. What will be relevant, impactful, simple, consistent and memorable to each different target audience may be slightly different.

Trying to appeal to everyone with one piece of communication is a guaranteed way to waste some of your already precious budget – be really clear whom you want to speak to and what you think they really think, feel and need to know. If you are a removal company why waste money putting leaflets through every letterbox telling of your removal service? Focus on those houses with Sold or Sale Agreed signs up.

I was reading some old notes from a course I did on advertising and came across the following adage (apologies to the source of this ditty, as I have no idea as to its roots and was probably created in the days of Conservative rule):

The Times is read by people who *run the country*
The Daily Mirror is read by people who *think they run the country*
The Guardian is read by people who *think they ought to run the country*
The Daily Express is read by people who *think the country ought to be run the way it used to be*
The Daily Telegraph is read by people who *think it still is*
The Daily Mail is read by the *wives of those who run the country*
The Financial Times is read by people who *own the country*
The Sun is read by people who *don't care who runs the country or who owns it, as long as she's got big ★★★★*

You must know who you're trying to speak to before choosing how to reach them.

Your communication could be aimed at current customers to tell them about a new service they can benefit from, at ex-customers to tell them why and how you have improved, at occasional customers to convince them to buy from you more often, at men to encourage them to buy your products as gifts for their partners, at women to tell them to buy for themselves or friends, at new customers to tell them who you are.

These decisions run hand in hand with knowing what you actually want to achieve (i.e. get ex-customers to start buying from me again) – what your objectives are.

WHAT ARE YOUR OBJECTIVES?

Ultimately, of course, your main objective is to get people to buy – to improve your sales and profits. Realistically though, can you make someone who has never heard of you or your company before buy from you with one just piece of communication (including a sales call)? If you are selling to other businesses, and especially if your products or services are either expensive or a major component of what they go on to produce, it will take some time and consistent communication to convince them to buy from you.

So, yes, the ultimate objective of all communication is to increase sales. But think of sales as your business objective. The objective of communication is to move customers along the buying process as shown in the diagram on p. 118 – to move them closer and closer to choosing what you have for sale.

If your target customers are *unaware* (have no idea that you even exist) then they will never buy from you. They may stumble across you by mistake one day, but that's a pretty risky strategy to rely on after all the trouble you've gone to so far in putting a great offer together.

Your job as a marketer here is to make your target market *aware* of you (realise you exist). You must proactively choose which tools to use to make these potential customers aware. The key here is impact. Will you advertise, hire a brass band, run around the street

The buying process

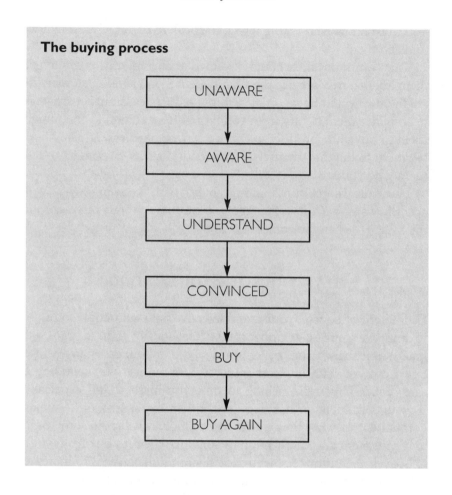

with a loudspeaker? If your attempts fail, the target market simply forgets about you and you're back to relying on people stumbling across you.

But you can't stop here – OK so people are aware that you exist – so what? Do they know what you have to offer, do they *understand* what you sell, how you sell and why you may be just what they are looking for to satisfy their needs? How are you going to make them understand? Will your shop window display make it clear? Will posters in the window? Will an advertisement? Will a feature in the local newspaper? What specific messages will you give potential customers about what you do? If your attempts at making people clearly understand who you are and what you do fail, again, you're unlikely to move them to buy from you.

Once people know who you are and what you do they may need to be *convinced* that you are the supplier for them. Why are you better than their current supplier? Why should they switch allegiance? What is it that makes you different? How will you get the evidence across to them? Unless you give them evidence that convinces them, then they won't believe your claims, and certainly won't actively choose to buy from you.

But if you do manage to convince them about your wares and source of competitive advantage, it's still not enough – how will you ensure that they now go on to make a purchase? How will you encourage them to *buy*? Which tools will you use to make your products or services really relevant to the individual needs of the potential customer? A sales demonstration? A workshop?

Great, they've bought! Hopefully, if you are a truly marketing-led business, your whole offer has been so customer oriented that the customer loves what you do and wants to buy from you again and again. Remember those competitors though – if I saw you successfully selling, then I'm very sure I'd try and get the customers back from you. So don't stop once customers have bought. What are you going to do to really make sure they *buy again*? How are you going to reinforce that they have made a good choice and will be satisfied? Have you ever bought a car or another high-value item and after spending many months making sure you're doing the right thing and choosing the right one, you take delivery and as soon as you get it home you wonder if you've made a mistake? Unless you get your customers out of this mindset then they may not buy again, no matter how expensive the item was. You must make sure you take action to reinforce the good choice they have made and encourage them to consider buying again when the time is right. And how will you reward their loyalty? Make sure you don't annoy your customers by using lots of money-off offers and promotions to attract new customers but give nothing to loyal customers to thank them for their custom. Will a letter thank them for their business? Will a demonstration showing all the extra things that come with the product and reminding them how they operate? Which tools should you use?

It is unlikely that one piece of communication can do all of these things. Some methods of communication are better than others at achieving particular objectives, so clarify what you are trying to do before rushing ahead and spending money on adverts or stands at trade fairs or direct mail leaflets.

For a business providing marketing learning to companies, I might do the following:

- Make aware – use current clients to spread my name to key contacts they have
- Understand – direct mail and invitation to a free workshop
- Convince – workshop to demonstrate my style and work done
- Buy – free delivery of a pilot programme
- Buy again – joint client internal brochure to advertise the course internally and attract participants.

A hotel or B & B may have advertised with the local Tourist Board which has raised awareness and generated interest. However, this may not be enough to encourage the potential customers to stay. Perhaps you need to show sample letters of praise from satisfied customers. Tell them to drop by to have a look around, show them a room/choice of rooms (you should be confident you have nothing to hide – if you have something to hide then you're not a marketing-led company).

So your communication objectives may be to: raise awareness, generate interest, generate a positive image, encourage trial, drive repeat sales and reward loyalty.

The next section looks at the different communication methods in more detail. It concentrates on advertising, public relations and direct marketing, giving guidelines and tips on using these methods.

COMMUNICATION METHOD SPECIFICS

Advertising

On TV, radio, national, regional or local newspapers, magazines, journals, buses, outdoor posters, on the Internet, on the rear of car park tickets or till receipts, hot-air balloons, aeroplane banners, on taxis, sandwich boards, sides of buildings, notice boards in the local library or local gym or newsagent's window, or on a huge board being pulled up the M1 behind a car, the choices open to you are huge.

Advertising involves paying to have your message placed on any of the media above. It costs you money from two angles – paying for the space you are taking and paying for the production of your message content, style and layout. Some smaller local publications, journals and brochures will have advertising departments who will handle both angles. All you need to provide is your words, any photos or layout ideas and, of course, the cash.

Before deciding to place an advertisement with anyone ask them for an advertisers' information pack. This will tell you not only costs involved and the deadlines for receipt of copy, but more importantly a breakdown of the audience who read/watch/listen/ attend. You can see instantly whether this is the right place to be advertising if you are to reach your target audience.

The price you will be quoted for an advertisement is what is known as the 'rate card'. Be aware that no one usually pays rate card. If you are a good negotiator or can show commitment to placing advertisementss in the future, you will certainly pay below rate card per advert. Make sure that any copy gets proofed – you should get to see and approve a final version before it is printed. That way you can avoid embarrassing adverts like the one I saw in a local newspaper advertising a Wedding Fair. Guests were invited to visit exhibitors' stands in all areas of wedding organisation, and enjoy free refreshments and 'canopies' – or maybe they meant marquees?

Public relations

Public relations (PR) enables you to enhance the positive image you have among your publics – customers, employees, investors and local communities. Rather than pay for the space for an advertisement on TV or radio or in press and magazines, you can send the media newsworthy *press releases* – information that will be of interest to their readers and viewers. They may decide to feature your 'news' in their media as editorial or news content. You may not get the same space an advertisement could have given you, but you will not have to pay for the editorial space, and readers/viewers may find the editorial content more believable than an advertisement and so it may be more effective.

Writing a press release is not an easy thing to do, especially if you are trying to do a hundred other things in your business. You may be better off using your time doing what you are good at and hire a PR specialist to write your releases. A good PR person will not only have press release writing skills, but also should have some great contacts with publications and key people and so increase the chances of your offer being featured. You should expect to pay around £250 per day as a fee, but shop around. If you feel you want to do it yourself, because after all you are the expert when it comes to your offer, then remember the following:

- why the article/story will be of interest to the media and their readers
- expect your article to be edited, summarised and altered before being featured
- therefore, stress the key message you want to get across – repeat, repeat, repeat this message in your original release
- send a sample or photograph with your release – that way they may show a picture in their article, or at least try the item and give a personal opinion (make sure you are really confident about the quality versus the competition and you are honest about the differentiation)
- stress what is particularly new or exciting about your offer.

Some people believe that in order to get good PR on local TV, radio or in the press and magazines you have to be an advertiser with them. This is not generally the case – in most instances it is different departments that deal with each. Secondly, and more importantly, if your news is really newsworthy, impactful, different, relevant and memorable then the media are going to be keen to use it to interest their audiences.

The Institute of Public Relations (020 7253 5151) runs a service called Matchmakers specifically for start up businesses. For a modest fee they will provide names of six PR experts in your area who are used to dealing with your line of work.

The Public Relations Consultants' Association runs a similar service (020 7233 6026). They also produce a useful booklet on how to find a good PR consultant.

If you choose a consultant who is a member of the IPR, they will be able to make use of a toolkit to prove value for money. They will analyse the coverage you are getting, and the enquiries and sales you are generating.

As PR is about generating good publicity, you could get an individual or celebrity or key opinion leader to endorse, or be seen to advocate your product or service. The section on 'Some ideas' looks more at this.

Exhibitions

You may be part of an industry that is well represented in various trade or customer fairs and exhibitions. You could take a stand at these exhibitions where you can demonstrate your offer, speak to prospective customers, entertain current customers and, of course, see what the competition are up to. But please please be aware that attending exhibitions can be very costly in terms of money and time. It is imperative that you check with the organisers which type of people come. Ask them to give you a breakdown of the attendee profile. Ask to be put in contact with previous exhibitors – get first-hand feedback from them on the value of attending. While you may feel that you can't afford not to be seen to attend, are you prepared to accept the presence of people who can't make decisions or who are just there for a day out? Be clear what your objectives are. Are you there to make contacts, or there to sell, or just raise awareness of your offer? I have many a 'fond' memory of spending 12 hours behind a stand at a Wine Fair where the majority of publicans, restaurateurs, and wine retailers seemed to be on a boozy day out – they certainly didn't seem to have any interest in any particular wine other than to ensure they tasted it, and again just to make sure. Come the next day most of them would have no idea which ones they preferred at all – on evaluating our attendance, our presence did nothing to gain new listings for the wines.

Even if you do decide not to take a stand then it may be worth while to go along anyway. You get to see what the competition are up to and can ask some pretty detailed questions of exhibitors, you get to see the type of attendee you could expect, and there's nothing to stop you observing the sort of interest that's being generated.

Sponsorship

There may be a team, person, activity or cause that you consider sponsoring. It is sometimes seen as PR, as the sponsorship generally enhances the positive image of your business. Sponsorship is more than paying money for your name to appear on the shirts, in the brochure, on the poster, although if this is all you want it to be then it can. In order to make sponsorship do more than just get aware-ness for your name, you should try to use it to move people to the next stage of the buying process at least – make them understand what it is you do. Are you able to obtain a membership list as part of the sponsorship deal and so communicate directly with each potential customer? Are you able to exhibit your products or provide details of your services at each sponsored event? Look beyond the initial sponsorship.

Direct marketing

Direct marketing is rather a broad term used to describe any direct communication with the customer: direct mail, home shopping, inserts, door-to-door, direct response adverts and telemarketing (both inbound, where customers call to get more information and outbound, where the company calls the customers). We will focus here on direct mail and door-to-door.

Direct mail is any information you send addressed to a specific individual (usually through the post, but by e-mail the principles are similar). Door-to-door is unaddressed but personally delivered through letterboxes.

A brochure and covering letter you send is direct mail, samples of your product through the letterbox is direct mail or door-to-door if unaddressed. Postcards from double glazing, house painting, home insurance, credit card and other such companies are direct mail or door-to-door. Monthly mailings from Air Miles are direct mail. A monthly pack from the *Sunday Times* Wine Club is direct mail. Your monthly credit card bills stuffed full of other offer leaflets is direct mail. That brochure from Britannia Music or Book Club who you stopped buying from years ago is direct mail. First Direct text messages to your mobile phone informing you that your salary has been paid into your current account is direct mail. A text message from Orange mobile phone Directory Enquiries confirming the telephone number you requested. These are all direct mail.

Gillette won a direct marketing award in 1997 for best use of door-to-door. They wanted users of competitors' cheap disposable razors to sample their SensorExcel system. With the objective being to grow market share the target market was, of course, not current Gillette disposable users, but non-Gillette users. They selected residential areas on a combination of profile information on purchasing habits. On day one, a yellow bag was left at houses, urging people to dispose of their disposables and join the shaving revolution. On day two interested customers were asked to hang the bags outside their homes, to be swapped for samples of SensorExcel. The campaign persuaded 800 000 people to try the new product – at the lowest cost per customer of any other campaign.

Unfortunately much direct mail and door-to-door is unkindly referred to as 'junk mail'. When is it really junk? When the wrong message is delivered to the wrong person – it goes back to the earlier point about relevance of the message to the target. It is interesting to note though that while only 20 per cent of advertisements are reported to be noticed, 77 per cent of direct mail is opened and 63 per cent read (even if it then goes on to be binned). However, it is fair to say that it can be expensive (it can cost around £1000 for every 1000 items you wish to mail by the time you acquire the names, produce the material and post it out or deliver it), it does not generate huge response rates (5 per cent is average – amazing that 95 per cent failure rate is deemed as acceptable!) and it relies hugely on the quality of the names and addresses used (maybe the overuse of the phrase junk mail comes from too many companies using poor quality lists).

However, I think there are many advantages and benefits of direct mail and door-to-door:

- it can be targeted, you can decide precisely who gets the mail and who doesn't, compared to scattered advertising there is little wastage
- direct mail can be personalised, which may be key in building relationships
- the message can be tailored right down to individual level if necessary in a way that advertising never can. ('Dear Mrs Russell, Hope you enjoyed test driving the new Renault. Sorry we didn't have more time and I hope you managed to collect your daughter from school on time.'), the recipient knows you are speaking only to them
- you are able to follow up direct and door-to-door mail – you can telephone everyone, non-respondents, respondents, with more information, thanks or questions
- compared to a poster or advertisement you can get detailed information across on direct and door to door mail
- compared to other methods direct mail is measurable. If you mail 1000 people and 100 respond you know the effectiveness – you can see which of them went on to buy
- you can test direct and door-to-door mail on a small basis before you spend lots of money mailing to a huge area – you could test different letters to see which people respond better to, whether coupons are good incentives, whether the list has a good chance of getting 5 per cent response
- you can optimise your timing so as people receive your mail and it prompts their purchase. Have you noticed how many fast-food menus come through your door on a Friday? A well-known cosmetic brand targeting teenage girls makes sure their mail is delivered on a Thursday which gives the girls time to discuss with their friends on the Friday, before buying on a Saturday
- it can be a good way to keep your plans and news hidden from the competition

Summary of the advantages and disadvantages of direct mail and door-to-door

Disadvantages	Advantages
Accuracy of mailing list	Targeted
Low response rate	Personalised
Image as junk mail	Tailored
	Can follow up
	Detailed information
	Measurable
	Testable
	Optimise timing
	Hide activity from competitor
	Build database

■ if you collect information on the individuals' responses then it is the start of a potential customer database for you, which will help you really understand customers

Ten Steps to Great Direct Mail

1. **Set your objectives**
   Be clear what you are trying to achieve. Be realistic too – because of the amount of mail people receive it may not work well as an awareness builder or interest generator. Although there are exceptions, direct mail tends to work better the further down the buying process you go.
2. **Set your budget**
   Plan for around 50p–£1 per mailing (more if giving away free samples or gifts).
3. **Identify the target audience**
   Are they potential, ex-, current, occasional or loyal customers? Describe them in detail – this makes point 4 easier. Make sure you can get the addresses of these people – do you have them already, do you know how you will get them or will you need to buy them from a list?
4. **Clarify the benefit**
   If you've done your research into customer needs or can be insightful then this can guarantee your message is relevant

and attractive to the target customers, e.g. some senior citizens don't have central heating so perhaps they'd love your café to offer a hot soup special on pension days in winter time.

5. **Develop the mailing**

   Write your covering letter and enclose anything else that may be relevant. Don't forget that the envelope is also part of the mailing. The next section gives some tips for developing a mailing.

6. **Test the mailing**

   Before you go ahead and spend money on a large mailing get some feedback – send it to one or two people who represent your target audience and get their feedback, or mail to a sample in a test area. This is especially important to check the quality of any list you may have bought.

7. **Mail at the right time**

   Make sure they receive the mailing at the best possible time to generate a response – remember the teenagers and make-up shopping at the weekend. Don't mail to anyone any more than monthly – you're pestering!

8. **Handle responses**

   Be prompt and efficient in your handling of any responses. If people want more information, call them immediately – strike while the iron is hot. If customers are waiting an information pack they requested, send it as soon as possible.

9. **Add information to database**

   If people tell you they don't want to be mailed again, act upon their request – otherwise you will send something that goes straight in the bin. Gather the information that will be relevant for future activity.

10. **Analyse responses**

    To help you plan for next time, always analyse the responses. Did you get a 2 per cent response rate or a 20 per cent response rate? Check with future customers to identify whether the mailing influenced purchase. If customer A has never ever responded to any of your mailings, ask if they wish to be removed from your list.

The mailing list

You may not have a list of people whom you wish to mail – perhaps you're looking for new customers.

Pick up any marketing magazine and you will find advertisements from companies who are list brokers or suppliers – they will sell or rent you a list of potential names. All you need to do is give them a specific profile – I want all working women under the age of 35 who have cats, or I want all families in the KT postcode region earning over £50K who have children in private education. The Royal Mail and *Yellow Pages* are both good places to go first for list help. Likewise many new small business service providers such as Clearlybusiness.com and BT.GetStarted all offer help in sourcing lists. (See Chapter 13, Places to go for help.)

Maybe you've received some direct mail already from companies offering a list service who have identified you as a new small business in need of a list of prospect customers – meet up with them, ask them why you should use them, why are they better, how up to date their lists are, how often do their lists get cleaned? The worst thing you can do is buy an old list.

In addition to mailing the right people, a key part of the effectiveness of any direct mail is the mailing itself. So here are some tips for putting together a mailing.

Putting together a mailing

Key tip – make it feel like personal mail, not a standard letter that everyone has received.

The envelope

■ Think of the envelope as you would do the packaging for your product. How could you use shape, colour, texture and graphics to give impact?

■ Why does it have to be an envelope at all? This could be an opportunity to stand out and be remembered.

■ Remember first impressions – get the name right and the label straight. One insurance company sent a letter to a Mr Whingeing Git, while an electrical store sent one to a Mrs Ugly Fat Cow – both the results of computer generated names and addresses input by annoyed sales staff having fun at the expense of 'troublesome' customers.

■ Could you have a teaser message on the envelope to encourage the recipient to at least open it?

■ Remember positioning – your direct mail must represent what you stand for be it professional, fun, serious, exciting, feminine, authoritative, innovative and so on.

The letter

■ Make sure, as with the envelope, it is not addressed to Mr P de File.

■ Most recipients go straight to the end of the letter to see who it's from, therefore make it someone important (significant sender).

■ People will also read a PS before they read any body of a letter, so restate the benefit you offer here.

■ The letter needs to be as easy to read as possible – use headings and paragraphs to break up the text, and *italics* or **bold** to highlight key messages.

■ Use short sentences and short paragraphs (especially the first) to keep people reading.

■ Remember you are writing to somebody, so write as if you can see them – consider your tone and style carefully, don't use jargon and if your targets are older people then consider using larger letters.

Contents of the envelope

■ Beware enclosing too much information

■ If you want people to get back to you then include a postage paid reply device.

Example of a bad direct mail letter

Ref No: 72059999999999999 / 1346

Mr A B Sample
1 Any Road
Any Town
Anyshire
AB1 1AB

14th June 1999

Dear Mr Sample

Customer feedback is critical for the continuation of our intent to maintain the ease of shop for our customers. I am sure that you understand how important feedback from someone like yourself is – improvements which have been implemented so far have come from such feedback.

We would appreciate if you could take the opportunity to provide us with your feedback in the areas of alcoholic beverages, cosmetics and medication, fruit and vegetables and pre-school children's products.

Should you reply, then to thank you for completing the questionnaire enclosed, we will enter your name into a prize draw and you could win £1000 worth of shopping vouchers. 50 runners up will win £50 shopping vouchers, 100 others will win £10 shopping vouchers, and 500 others will receive a voucher to redeem against a product in-store up to the value of £5. Please ensure that your response is received by us by 15th July 1999 in order to ensure entry.

Thanking you in advance for your reply

Yours sincerely

Ms Elizabeth Tennant
CRT Manager

A bit of an exaggeratedly bad letter to send – very formal, fancy words used rather than simple sentences, a huge intimidating first paragraph, jargon instead of language a customer would use (alcohol, health and beauty, fruit and veg, toddlers are better words), the incentive to reply is confusing and likely to turn off anyone, no summary, what on earth is a CRT Manager? It reads like a computer-generated, non-personal, bog standard letter.

Opposite is an example of an extremely cleverly done direct mail letter developed by participants on a course I ran – would any company be brave enough to send this I wonder?

Sales promotions

For end customers or for trade customers you can incentivise purchase and encourage sales through short-term special offers. Offers such as supermarket club points to reward your loyalty are now so long term that they are not a sales promotion, but part of their core offer. By sales promotion we mean everything you see in the diagram on p. 134. The only limits to the variety of sales promotion on offer are your creativity and of course the law. (So check with the Institute of Sales Promotion for what you can and can't do or say.)

There is no doubt that further down the buying process, sales promotion techniques can drive trial and purchase of your product or service, and through loyalty promotions or bulk buying schemes protect repeat purchase against competitors. However, be aware that sales promotions are only short term, there is no guarantee that once your promotion is over the customer won't go back to buying the product he used to buy, or that she will ever buy your product or service again. Be aware that sometimes promotions become so expected that people stop buying when your product or service is not on offer. Be aware that you could be giving money off to people who were going to buy the product or service anyhow, so all you have done is dilute your profit. Be aware that promotions attract 'switchers': promiscuous customers who have little loyalty to anyone and simply shop around for the best deal. Be aware of the effect on your image if you are constantly seen to be on promotion.

6 Millington Road
Hayes
Middlesex
UM3 4AY

16th June 1999

Card no. 1212134343434345665

Ms Lynn Moffat
The Node Conference Centre
Codicote
Hertfordshire
NO17 6HF

We kidney you not . . .

Dear Lynn,

Great news! We've raised the **steaks** and got **tongues** wagging on our meat departments.

You recently told us you thought our meat was **offal** and we've listened to what you had to say. We've **beefed** up our range and introduced 60 new fresh meat products which we're sure will **liver** up to your expectations!

With 20 new cuts of meat, 15 new poultry products and 10 new additions to our Meat of the World range, we think we've really got to the **heart** of the problem.

In the same vein, our ethnic foods have **korma** long way and we've added 15 Thai, Moroccan and Indonesian lines to our range – they're all **veally** good!

We've trained specialist butchery staff in all our stores who'll be happy to chew the **fat** with you and won't **mince** their words when it comes to sorting out your meal solutions.

So come on, we'd love you to be **chicken** up on us! We promise that all our offers are **kosher**. After all, would we tell you **porkies**?

Yours **skincerely,**

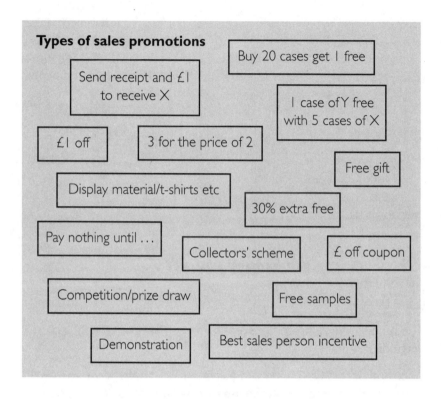

Types of sales promotions

- Buy 20 cases get 1 free
- Send receipt and £1 to receive X
- 1 case of Y free with 5 cases of X
- £1 off
- 3 for the price of 2
- Free gift
- Display material/t-shirts etc
- 30% extra free
- Pay nothing until …
- Collectors' scheme
- £ off coupon
- Competition/prize draw
- Free samples
- Demonstration
- Best sales person incentive

Do you remember the Hoover fiasco of 1992? Hoover was offering two free return flights to Europe or America if anyone purchased any Hoover washing machine or household appliance worth more than £100. The company expected such a generous offer to attract many, but thought they may be put off by strict conditions in the small print. Undeterred, they received a huge response and had difficulty honouring the offer. It was a financial and PR disaster for Hoover.

So long as you are aware of the dangers and drawbacks of, and plan any sales promotions with them in mind, they can have a role to play in incentivising purchase.

It is September, and if you're a bit of a secret Alan Titchmarsh or Charlie Dimmock then you'll know it's time to get your daffodil bulbs in if you want some colour in your garden in the early part of next year. There's a local garden centre near me: Squires, quite well known and reputed among gardeners I'm told. They realise that much of the sales in a garden centre come from impulse and attraction while wandering around. If they can get you in to buy anything, even if it's just a few daffodil bulbs, they might encourage you to splash out on some tulips too! They also want to make sure that the gardener doesn't buy bulbs from the supermarket, thinking it's easier. They must give people a reason to pop in again. So, having just bought a house with a small garden, and knowing nothing about gardening other than that daffodils are yellow and the bulbs should be planted now, their promotion in the local newspaper caught my eye. Inside the newspaper was a paper bag, clearly branded from Squires. On visiting Squires you can fill the bag with daffodil bulbs for only 25p. It is a very clever sales promotion. Once I get to the garden centre I'll probably want more bulbs. In fact it gets me to look round the garden centre and probably increase my basket spend beyond my planned level.

Personal selling

In the midst of all the sexy advertising, exciting PR, creative direct mail and immediately effective sales promotions you can implement, one of the key methods of communication sometimes gets forgotten – the salesperson. Personal selling to customers and prospects will be important at some stage in order actually to sell the products or services you have. To reflect its importance a complete section in Chapter 7 is dedicated to it.

We've established the need to stand out against all the clutter of communication that exists. You do not need a huge budget to do this. Remember you're looking to be relevant to quite a specific target audience – so here are some ideas you could adopt.

SOME IDEAS

Use innovative channels

You'll probably remember the dreadful news about pathologists at a Liverpool hospital who stripped organs from children's bodies without parental consent. Over 100 000 organs and body parts were stored at hospitals around the country. The scandal had the unfortunate but not surprising effect of discouraging parents offering organs of their children should they die. Many children desperate for transplants are at risk. Keen to encourage parents not to fear donating organs the NHS looked for a way to communicate donor cards – an impactful way. What would be almost guaranteed to be looked at? Monthly payslips – they issued donor cards in the envelope the payslip arrived in. It will be interesting to see the results.

Why have I used this story? Sometimes you need to think differently about how to reach your target audience – don't go down the usual advert in trade magazine, press release route. Being innovative may help you stand out and be remembered. One technique to help you do this is to think about the life of your target customer across the 24 hours of a typical day.

Go through their day from the moment they get up to the moment they go to bed and visualise what they do minute by minute and hour by hour. This is where you can reach them – listening to the radio driving to work, buying a snack in the canteen at lunchtime, going to the gym on the way home may identify the opportunities to use local radio advertising, brand napkins or cups in the canteen, put posters on notice boards, sponsor the squash league or brand the treadmill electronic display. Médecins sans Frontiers postcard caught my eye in the gym recently. 'Blow £1000 on Drugs.' I wondered what on earth they could possibly be communicating. Simple, impactful and consistent with the MSF image of being controversial in their approach to Third World Aid this postcard caught the people MSF expected to donate in places where they knew they would be.

Get current customers to recommend you

Word of mouth is the cheapest and most credible form of advertising and communication you can encourage. If you have really pleased your customers you may find that you don't even need to encourage them – they naturally advocate your business. However, people share bad experiences more than good, so don't rely on advocacy automatically – encourage it. That's why music, book and video clubs give free products to members who enlist other members. That's why campsites in France give cases of wine to families who sign up new holidaymakers.

If you are a house removals company, send a 'Welcome to your new home' postcard a couple of weeks after you've helped them move in. Tell them you hope they're happy and were pleased with your service. Ask if they'd be kind enough to pass on your name and information to someone they know may need your services in the future.

If you're a photographer or printer you could offer a free reprint or enlargement or a discounted repeat print run to anyone who recommends you to a friend who goes on to place an order.

Personal trainers could offer clients a reduced price session in return for introducing someone who becomes a customer.

The local riding stables where you've gone religiously for the last two years could offer a free horse ride in return for constantly bringing friends to the riding school.

Give prospect customers the name of a loyal customer who would be happy to tell them about your offer: perhaps the loyal customer would be prepared to be quoted in any promotional material you produce.

Get experts or people in authority to recommend you

With so much customer cynicism regarding advertising, and unfortunate experiences with cowboy companies on the increase, make sure that if there is a governing body or association linked with your industry that you are recognised by it. The Internet is . making it easier for customers to find out whether companies are reputable and endorsed by associations.

We briefly made reference to the power of endorsement by authority figures in the PR specific section. Tom Cruise in *Top Gun* did wonders for Ray Bans. Delia Smith's recommendation of eggs and cranberries did overnight what the egg and cranberry growers associations would probably have never achieved through advertising. By simply recommending a Lunapan as *the* pan with which to make omelettes, orders for the small company increased from 200 to 9000 per year – a complete nightmare rather than welcome sales boost I shouldn't wonder.

The growth in eating and drinking out, and being seen in the right places, has proved to be a big opportunity for drinks and bars. Get the coolest bar in town to recommend your drink, music, décor, whatever. Get the coolest celeb in town to be seen using, drinking, listening, lounging, using your product or service.

Most target markets have a magazine that is aimed at them and will cover content relevant to your offer. Send details and a sample of your product and press release to the editor (find the name of the editor in *BRAD*, British Rate and Data, in any library) and hope they feature it – *Ideal Home, BBC Good Food* etc, – they are trying to offer great service to their customers too! Get these magazines or press articles to recommend your website.

Volunteer to talk at a forthcoming conference or event where your credibility will be enhanced – it's also a great networking opportunity.

Of course the power of people in authority works the other way too – all it takes is for them to deem your product the biggest social *faux pas* among your customers and their peers and sales and image suffer just as much. Jeremy Clarkson's penchant for wearing Levi's did their image nothing but harm among the core target market of cool teenagers and trendies.

Get related companies to recommend you

Removal companies could link with estate agents. In the home-buyers pack that gets sent by the estate agent to clients is included a list of recommended local companies for removals, storage, taxis in the area, good pubs and restaurants, etc.

If you are a mobile DJ or band or photographer or cakemaker, etc., then carefully consider all the venues in your area that get used for weddings and parties. Does the venue recommend businesses such as yours to people booking events? If so how do you get on that list? If not, encourage the hotel to recommend you – it's a way of helping the venue offer a better service to their potential guests. If the venue needs to be sure that you are a credible and reliable supplier before they recommend you, invite them to other events where you are performing, or get happy previous guests to endorse you. Are you able to pass a percentage of your nightly rate to the venue in return for recommending you?

If you run riding stables, leave leaflets in local hotel receptions. They may display them for free in a bid to be seen to offer customers a great choice of things to do. Alternatively you could offer a gift to the hotel every time staff send guests to go riding – a free 1 hour ride to a member of staff. As a reciprocal the riding school could recommend the hotel as a place to stay.

I spent Christmas last year in a hotel in Scotland with my new (and I hasten to add first and only) husband. As with many Scottish hotels that cater for a mainly foreign tourist trade at this time of the year (and for the purposes of my story then please forgive me for including anyone who is not Scottish in the definition of foreign), part of their package of festivities was to include malt whisky tasting, Scottish dancing lessons, stories on the history of Scotland and kilt wearing, and a Boxing Day ceilidh (just realised that the following explanation could be construed in many ways – men in kilts, a band playing fiddles and accordions, ladies in various states of dress, lots of Gay Gordon's, Dashing White Sergeant's and Draps o'Brandy, spinning, singing, hooching and tscheuching, and generally dancing until exhausted). Christmas Day evening saw the Scottish tartan and kilt tales followed the next afternoon by malt whisky tasting. Well, partly due to brilliant presence and presentation by the speaker, and coupled with the atmosphere and celebrations, I have never seen so many foreigners rush to reception and ask where they could hire a kilt to wear to the ceilidh (which by this time was due to take place in around five hours). I couldn't help but think what a brilliant opportunity it could have been for a local kilt hire (or sale) business. Unfortunately at such short notice, and on one of the main public holidays of the year, the search for kilts was fruitless. Perhaps local kilt companies could keep in touch with their local hotels and get a calendar of future events from them. That way they'd have advance notice of when likely business may come in. The hotel wants to ensure it offers a great stay to its guests, so perhaps they'd be willing to send their guests up to your local place of business to get 'kitted out'. Perhaps the hotel would be willing to put one of your brochures in each bedroom guest directory. Maybe you could offer an hour of kilt-dressing as part of the hotel's programme of events at which you could take along a range of sizes and colours for guests to try on. Having felt the glory of being dressed in such finery the guests may wish to hire for the ceilidh. It would give you some advance notice. However, if working on Christmas Day and Boxing Day were a big no-no with your family perhaps the hotel would act as kilt hirer on your behalf? You could deliver a range of stock to the hotel before the Christmas break and having agreed terms of hire and return, have them manage the process. (I'm assuming here you will have a good relationship with the hotel if it is local to you, and a good relationship with key staff in the hotel, whom you trust to manage the hiring process.)

Reward your loyal customers

Your aim with your loyal customers is to keep them loyal. (Of course, don't forget there may be some loyal customers who you wish were not customers at all. Some customers you might profit from losing. If they cost you too much to deal with, do not actively try to retain them.)

There is a danger that your loyal customers may get annoyed with all the 'special deals' that you do to attract new customers. As an M&S account card holder I used to get livid at being approached in-store by staff telling me that if I signed up for an account card today I'd get £25 M&S vouchers free. I got nothing for choosing to become an account card holder, and here you are telling me that those who are not will get £25 vouchers! It's like having a mortgage and after months and years of faithfully repaying loan and interest you see that new customers are being given £1000 cash back. I think people do expect it to happen a bit more nowadays; it's the luck of when you struck the deal, but it still does nothing to lock customers on to you and keep them loyal.

Don't ignore your current customers (don't assume they'll stay with you once you've got them, especially if they see that there are prizes to be won by being promiscuous and switching suppliers every so often). Someone can always offer a better deal. Not everyone can improve the rewards you get in return for the loyalty you give.

That's why today you see M&S holding special open evenings, tastings and demonstrations for account card holders. That's why Harrods give account card holders an extra 10 per cent off sale prices on certain days. That's why Bosch hold special DIY days for £99 so the target market can receive tips from experts on DIY and using power tools. That's why Land Rover hold off-road driving events for owners whose most off-road experience is hitting the camber or a pot hole in badly surfaced roads. So think about what you can do for loyal customers that they know is unique. Previews of new stock, discounted call out charges, first refusal on limited stocks, invitations to discussions with experts, newsletters with up to the minute advice and suggestions.

Re-attract lapsed and ex-customers

If you insist on using direct mail, please don't bombard lapsed and ex-customers with it – if you know they still live at that address but they haven't replied to any of your attempts to get them to ask you leave them alone, delete them from your list. *Hello* magazine have mailed me six times to tell me the subscription I bought for my mum for Christmas is about to end/about to end/ended/ ended/ended for some time now/nearly time to get another for Christmas. Direct mail will not encourage me to take out another subscription.

Maybe an ex-customer needs proof that you have improved. You may need to communicate improvements in your offer, offer a discount to encourage them to trial again or invite them along to see and experience your improvements.

Perhaps the customers have just forgotten about you. Write to them and tell them you'd love to hear from them again and remind them what you have to offer.

EVALUATING YOUR COMMUNICATION

There is absolutely no point spending money on different communication methods if you don't know whether they are successful. If an advert designed to generate sales, costing £1000 last month generated no sales enquiries then there's little point placing the same advert again, even if you manage to negotiate the bargain price of £500 – beware that logic.

Ask around as part of your research which methods your friends and other businesses have used effectively. Think as a customer which communication has had an effect on you. When there's a sudden rush on a certain product or service you offer have you asked customers why they're buying that one?

If you used PR, how much coverage did you manage to generate? Have you noticed a difference in sales or enquiries following the coverage of your story? If you used advertising, have you noticed a difference in sales or enquiries? If you send a brochure out to people, keep a note of who they are. Call them up to check they received it. Ask if they have any questions. Track them to see if they go on to buy from you. How many of the 2000 people you mailed have responded? Call up a random sample of those who didn't and ask if they'd mind giving you some feedback – why were they not interested?

Ask people what in particular they liked or disliked about your communication – the only way to plan effective communication activity is to use your learning from the past and your insight into your customers.

SUMMARY CHECKLIST

- You need to reach the right people at the right time with the right message
- Great communication is relevant to the audience, has impact, is simple, is consistent with the rest of the marketing mix, and is memorable

- Which method of communication to use depends on your budget, objectives and target audience
- The buying process is a good way to think about your objectives and which methods will be best to use
- Ensure advertising reaches the specific audience without wastage
- PR is good for credibility – people are less cynical of independent endorsement
- Direct mail depends on the quality of names on your list
- Sales promotion can generate short-term sales, but consider the long-term effects
- Use innovative channels
- Get current customers to recommend you
- Get experts or authority to recommend you
- Get related companies to recommend you
- Reward loyal customers
- Re-attract lapsed or ex-customers
- Evaluate whether your communication has been successful.

7
Buying and Selling

Selling has to be the most exciting thing
you can do with your clothes on.
John Fenton

THE CHAPTER AT A GLANCE

Chapter 6 explained the importance of communication of your offer to potential customers in order to gain a sale. One of the key methods of communication is of course 'personal selling'. This chapter looks at the role of the salesperson in the marketing mix and some ways to ensure successful selling.

Most small companies don't go out of business because they fail to make a profit, but because of cash flow problems – you're not selling enough or your customers' aren't paying on the one hand, yet on the other your suppliers are demanding immediate payment. Therefore this chapter will look at you both as a customer buying from suppliers, and also as a supplier selling to customers. It is a chapter designed to whet the appetite and will only skim the surface of the buying and selling process. Both are core skills your business needs in order to compete especially in difficult times.

BUYING FROM SUPPLIERS

No matter the business you are in, at some point you will deal with suppliers – people who want to sell to you – advertising space, temporary or permanent staff, business cards, letterheads, design services, employer's insurance, new product ranges, ingredients, raw materials, utilities such as gas, electricity, telephone services, water, etc.

Dealing with suppliers is a really good opportunity to think about what they do and how they do it – and to compare it to how your business acts as a supplier to your customers. Being in the shoes of a customer really brings home to you insight into how your customers might feel dealing with you.

It is an opportunity to spot something they do particularly well, perhaps that attracted you as a customer in the first place, and apply it to your business and your customers. It is also an opportunity to spot things they do badly or that annoy you and make sure you don't find yourself repeating their mistake with your customers.

Your suppliers, the people you buy from, may also be selling to large businesses: businesses with purchasing departments and accounts payable departments. I guarantee they will have experienced frustrations, late payment of bills, constant chasing money, last minute demands and inflexible 'by-the-book' purchasers. (I think they like to be called 'procurement specialists' now). The result of the above is that the supplier doesn't like doing business with them, does the minimum they need to keep the business and does his best but doesn't go out of his way to be resourceful or innovative. This is great news for smaller businesses.

As a supplier how do you get treated? Which of your customers do you like dealing with? I bet you go out of you way to be more helpful to the customers you like and I bet you do much more for the nice ones. So make your suppliers love working with you.

How important are the goods and services you buy from each supplier to the quality of your end offer? What percentage of the total cost of your offer do you buy in from suppliers? The more you rely on the quality and price of the supplier's product in your end offer the more reason to make them love dealing with you. Imagine a florist being let down by a supplier of arum lilies the very day the promotion on arum lilies is due to start. Imagine a convenience store being let down by the newspaper or milk supplier who decided to send their scarce stock to customers of higher importance to them. When the suppliers and their products and services are really important then you can't afford for them not to supply you, provide erratic quality, deliver late or price inconsistently.

Even supplies which you could do without (they don't really affect the quality of your customer offer) or which account for a tiny percentage of your total running costs (business cards for example), you never know when you may need a favour, or help at short notice, or a shorter than usual print run. Just because a supplier is not that important to you does not mean you should treat them any less well.

HOW AND WHY TO MAKE SUPPLIERS LOVE YOU

How to be a pleasure to deal with:

- say thank you every now and again, especially if they have gone out of their way to help you
- don't see the payment of the bill as the thank you
- speak to everyone in the company with the same courtesy and enthusiasm as you do the chief
- speak to them like people – take an interest in what they do
- keep them informed of any changes to orders or specifications, do not wait until you take delivery and then complain it isn't right
- try to give people as much notice as possible
- put yourself in their shoes and treat them as you would expect or like a customer to treat you.

Why you should be a pleasure to deal with:

- they're more likely to do you favours
- they'll go the extra mile for you
- they'll put in 110 per cent
- you'll have them thinking about how to help you even when they're not working
- they'll treat you like a partner in a relationship rather than a one night stand
- they'll approach you first with propositions which could be to your long-term benefit.

HOW IMPORTANT ARE
YOU TO YOUR SUPPLIERS?

If you account for only 1 per cent of a supplier's business, it's fair to say that you're not that important to them – unless they see you as a star company in the future that they want to start developing a relationship with now. If you're not that important to them, then don't expect to get the best prices or best service around. (You can't rely on them having read this book.) Even by being a pleasure to deal with you won't be in as strong a negotiating position as a business more important to the continued success of the supplier.

As a small business you will be at an immediate cost disadvantage when it comes to buying from most suppliers. Expect them to be giving large discounts off their list prices to big companies, in return for a large and, in their eyes, consistent guarantee of volume. There are four things I'd suggest when in this situation.

Firstly, realise your importance and don't expect to get the same low prices large businesses get. If you can, find out exactly how much of the supplier's business you account for – it may put you in a better bargaining position. Ask your supplier who else they deal with – you may find you are more important than you think.

Secondly, if you really don't like dealing with a huge and powerful supplier (in spite of all the pluses that may bring – regular supply, wide ranges, innovative products, expertise), look for smaller suppliers who will treat you as a more important customer. If the only reason you are moving to a smaller supplier is on the basis of price, ensure you will not lose out on other areas – flexibility, range, regular supply, etc.

Thirdly, network with other small businesses to compare suppliers. Ask who gives them great service. Ask who they like dealing with.

Fourthly, join a club which will buy on your behalf. There are several companies who pool together individual or small company orders and in return get better prices for you than you'd get buying as a small business. Usecolor.com, for example, offer better deals on stationery and office equipment for the small companies who are monthly subscribers to their website and service.

In short, make yourself important to a supplier.

SOME TIPS FOR
DEALING WITH SUPPLIERS

Even if you can prove you are going to be a customer of the future whom they cannot afford to ignore, some suppliers may ask to see credit references or a trading record before agreeing to supply you. As a small new business it may be highly unlikely for you to have such things, but don't take the request personally; they're just protecting their cash flow. What you need to do is work to prove your credit worthiness to them – get references from other suppliers, offer to pay gradually, negotiate a price for a full order, but take delivery of it piece by piece, paying it off gradually as received. This may be a situation where being part of a purchasing club could help. Ensuring customers are not a credit risk is sound business practice that you should also operate.

Keep records of all prices agreed with suppliers. Ask them to confirm them in writing, or confirm to them what you agreed. On receipt of the invoice check the figures are as agreed and the goods are as ordered. If there are errors, treat it as a mistake the first few times – then go elsewhere. If they are ripping you off, make sure you tell other companies about your experiences, and make sure you ask other businesses about theirs.

Suppliers generally are not out to rip you off, although one or two unscrupulous characters may slip through the net. If you think every supplier is out to 'do' you, just remember that you are also a supplier – are your customers going around thinking you are out to 'do' them? Just be vigilant – networking helps share experiences and remember customers share bad experiences more than good. One small business has recently successfully taken several printing companies to court for illegally operating a price-fixing cartel – when yet another printer in his local area quoted the exact price for a print job that all others had quoted, his suspicions were raised.

Finally, it's common practice in business to 'entertain, wine and dine' your customers either as a thank you for their business or to court them initially (which incidentally many big customers have put an end to for fear of it being seen as unethical or even 'bribery' on the part of the supplier). I suppose it's human nature to either see it as a thank you or to feel suspicious that somebody wants something in return – even if that's not the case at all. So turn it around – if a great relationship with a supplier is so important then why not entertain them? Suppliers are less likely than customers to assume there's a hidden agenda.

THE ROLE OF SELLING IN
THE CUSTOMER BUYING PROCESS

We mentioned in Chapter 6 that a key way to communicate with customers to lead them to buy is not just through advertisements, PR, direct mail or promotional offers, but also through the sales contact with your business. Advertising can lead a horse to water, while the selling can make it drink.

Remember the buying process discussed in Chapter 6 – an advertisement can raise awareness of the offer, PR can generate interest in it, direct mail might convince me further, but it may be the salesperson at the point of purchase who influences my buying decision. That influence could be positive or negative – if I get to the point of purchase, meet the salesperson, don't like him or his approach, then, unless I am desperate, it certainly reduces the chances of me buying.

I know someone who used to be a Mercedes salesman. He said it was the easiest car in the world to sell because customers who he spoke to usually took little convincing about the merits of Mercedes – they were aware of the cars, interested enough to consider buying one and convinced as to its benefits. It was just a case of which dealer and which deal they could get. All the salesman had to do was get them to the 'buy' part, perhaps through a test drive, and make sure the customer at least liked him.

Contact with a salesperson, where effective, can really draw a potential customer towards the sale – it starts the formation of a relationship. Many businesses reckon that one of the disadvantages of the Internet is that it removes the need for contact to be made with a salesperson at all and so the potential sale may be lost. Rather than speak to a salesperson who can start the relationship, the customer simply looks at the internet, finds what they need to (if they can) and leaves with what he needs (or not). Selling has a key role to play in the buying process. In order for the selling approach to be effective there are many things to consider, as detailed in the next section.

THINGS TO CONSIDER IN SELLING

Time

Successful selling may depend upon the time of year or the time of month that you speak with the prospective customer, especially if that customer is another business, or if the item is of high value. If you reach a company at the start of their financial year, they may be slightly less price sensitive than towards the end. It doesn't matter how effective the salesperson – if the customer's budget is zero then you may not sell anything. Think of your local councils – you can always tell when it's year-end and they need to use up their budgets (if they don't they might not get it all next year again) – road works everywhere. If the councils need the work done by the end of April they will buy from contractors who are able to do the job within the time frames set – the choice to buy may be based on a tender process and not on any selling skills of the contracting companies.

Company policy

If you are selling to another company, successful selling may depend on that company's policies of the moment. For example, if a company policy is to buy from a local supplier to support local farmers, no matter your salesperson skills, if you are not a local supplier then your sale will not be effective. If the customer is a large plc who has committed to the City £1 billion cost savings by the end of the year, they are going to be extremely sensitive to increases in expenditure – no matter the skill of the salesperson. Company policy may be to buy on tender documents only with a heavy price focus – a great salesperson may be of limited effect.

Reason for purchase

Successful selling may depend on understanding and tapping quickly in to the real reason why the customer is thinking of buying. If you understand that, you are more likely to say the right things and push the right buttons. For example, a buyer may buy the product or service provider that can provide the most kudos to him and his business – the best salesperson in the world may find it hard to overcome this if the customer does not perceive they can offer the same kudos. Other customers may buy because they see it as best for the company, others may consider long-term benefits, others may base the purchase on short-term factors such as price.

Product vs. service

You may need a different approach if selling a product to that for selling a service. Some people can put a value on £4500 and justify spending it on a new kitchen for the office staff, but may not be able to value or justify spending £4500 for the services of a project manager overseeing computer installation.

Type of buyer

It is important to remember that you sell to people. Perhaps you sell direct to the customer, or perhaps you sell to other companies. In the latter instance you do not sell to companies – you sell to individuals in companies. You need to hit the right buttons of each individual customer/buyer if the sale is to be successful. Everyone needs to know the benefits, but the benefits which turn on some buyers are different to those motivating to others. Some customers need to be excited and need the salesperson to make them feel excited. Some people are very rational and analytical and need detail, facts, proof, figures and information from every single supplier, not just your information, before they will make a decision. Some people are very pragmatic and want all the information, but need it to be condensed and summarised and the main benefits to them highlighted. Some people like doing something good for others and may need that proof demonstrated – 'What good will this do?' They base their decision on emotion rather than rationality. They'll buy from someone they like. Others, like my husband, base their buying decisions on completely emotional factors. They may like the salesperson, they buy what they see when they see it without necessarily checking all the alternatives, they may buy to feel good, or for prestige. They dislike people they see as 'smarmy salespeople trying to con me into buying' – they like to feel that they bought rather than were sold to.

Hit the wrong buttons and the sale will fail. Good salespeople say that they can instinctively tell which type of buyer someone will be within a few minutes of speaking to them. Ask them questions and see whether they respond with analytical or emotion-based answers – it will help you determine which approach to take with them. Chapter 12 talks about motivating people around you. Some of the suggestions given in that chapter are equally applicable to selling – you need to tap into what motivates someone if you are to move them to buy.

Presentation skills

You should treat the selling process as though it were a presentation – a presentation requiring you to influence the audience to buy. Chapter 11 discusses the presentation of your ideas and will explain in detail how to go about preparing and delivering a presentation to different audiences – read it as though your audience is a customer if you wish. The requirements are the same in a sales presentation as in any other – you need to grab attention, hold interest throughout, handle any questions or solve any problems the audience has, and bring it to a conclusion (in this case to close the sale).

I recently went into Boots Eye Clinic in Regent Street, London to enquire about Laser Eye Surgery (I'm blind and vain, what can I say?). The 'salesperson' sold me very few benefits, focusing on the features of the process. The benefits she did tell me were so technical that I completely switched off and didn't listen to a word she said. I wanted to hear that the process would be quick and painless, with little chance of failure. I wanted to know how quickly I would be able to see and to be shown how clear everything would look. Instead I was told about the NASA-type technology behind the laser. Yes it may be an important part of the process – but it wasn't an important part to me.

Deciding whether to be rational or emotional, dynamic or thorough goes hand in hand with having identified the type of buyer you are selling to – have a look at Chapter 11.

Finding new customers

Successful business relies on retaining customers, but on starting your business that's not very helpful. You need to be able to identify and find the right prospect customers. Telephoning or knocking on the doors of people you don't know or who have never had contact with you or your business before – cold calling – can psychologically destroy all but the most hardened of characters. Cold calling rejection rates are extremely high. In trying to make the cold call less cold, finding new customers requires you to take a more focused approach.

The start point is, of course, the description of your target market – the types of customers for whom your business has developed its offer. Having a clear description of your target customers helps avoid a random shotgun approach to finding people who'll buy. Remember the offer has been developed to meet the needs of your target market – if the offer is differentiated and 'ahead of the game' then the target customer in theory shouldn't need a really hard sell. Where you find a sell very difficult it may be that you have approached someone with different needs to your core target market – the offer was not developed for them. Focus on the target market.

Where you can, get referrals from contacts you have and at least a name or an introduction from someone. Ensure that you have used other communication tools to introduce yourself and your offer to the customer – make sure it's not a cold call.

Consider carefully the use of lists or directories – make sure they are up to date. As mentioned in Chapter 6 on communication in the direct mail section, you can buy lists of names of potential customers. Sometimes you only get their addresses, but for business lists (and in business directories which you can buy) you will get name, position, address and telephone details. Check in libraries, or with any relevant associations, which directories exist – if up to date they could be a good start point. But remember: try not to make the contact a cold one – do not expect a call to a person from a list to be any more effective than a random call. To find companies who sell or rent lists you could buy a copy of *Marketing Week* and look at the adverts appearing every week. Check *Yellow Pages* too, 'Database Services' is part of *Yellow Pages*. Ask colleagues and other businesses which list-companies they have used and how successful they were.

Buying situation

The buying situation could be a straightforward reorder of previous goods (staples or paper) or could be a completely new product or service they have never had before – one that may be complex or expensive (a new computer system). The skills required for each situation need to be considered carefully. Be aware of the concerns and difficulties a buyer faces in choosing complex and expensive new goods compared to reordering previous supplies.

Successful selling also relies on understanding just how important you are to the customer – can they get what you offer from another supplier? Be aware of your bargaining power in this buying situation.

CLOSING THE SALE

You may have hit every button of the customer, you may have presented brilliantly and tapped into the real needs of the buyer, but they may not have said, 'Yes, I want to buy' – you still need to close the sale. Customers, too, feel uncomfortable during decision-making and closing can be hard for both you and that customer. You need to make it as easy as possible for them to buy.

That means having enough checkouts and assistants to deal with every customer – or they may change their mind and walk away. It means reassuring them that they are about to make the right decision. It means detailing when you can supply and deliver and when the customer can be using the product or service. Ask them if delivery by Wednesday would be soon enough. Ask them if they'd like to fill out the paperwork now. Sometimes you don't need to be direct, and sometimes you have to be.

SUMMARY CHECKLIST

- Learn from what your suppliers do well and badly and think about it when you are dealing with your customers
- As a small business you may not be that important to some suppliers. They will do more for you if you make them love working with you
- Consider joining a buying consortium who can use their power to negotiate cheaper prices on some materials and services.
- Ask around to find who is good to deal with
- Successful selling depends on the ability of the salesperson to hit the right buttons in each customer
- But successful selling also depends on factors outside their control – time, customer policies, buying situations
- Finding new customers requires a focused approach in order to minimise the rejection that comes with cold calling.

8

The Art of Customer Service

Thank you for calling. In order for us to serve you better enter your account number now, followed by the star key. Thank you. For enquiries press *30. For product updates press *70 now. To reach a customer service operator press 29# now. Please press *#2 to hear a busy signal. Please press *001 to hear really bad music, hold for another 3 minutes and then be cut off.

THE CHAPTER AT A GLANCE

This chapter is the final one that focuses on an element of the marketing mix – the people and service element. The people element of your marketing mix can make a world of difference to your offer. The service you and your staff give can be the thing that differentiates you from the competition.

Good service is hard to define, because as we've frequently mentioned, customers want different things – what one person thinks is good service another may find average or even completely unacceptable. The manner in which you handle any complaints can have a huge effect on the perception that customers will have of your business, whether they will remain loyal to you and what they will tell their friends about you. Bad words spread quickly.

The chapter highlights the importance of good service, looks at what we mean by good and, of course, bad service, and suggests an approach to recovery from customer complaints.

THE IMPORTANCE OF CUSTOMER SERVICE

Customer service is important and becoming increasingly so. Service can be the differentiator between an average experience and a great one. Customers increasingly want to feel individual, important and listened to. Expectations of service levels are increasing – the more we receive good service in one experience the more we expect it in all. Bad service is the main reason for customers deserting companies – much more than price. On top of all this customers are being encouraged to complain more, to stand up for their rights, not to accept shabby service. Therefore the cycle of increasing expectations in service levels and complaint handling continues.

If you satisfy a customer, then they may tell 3–5 friends about you. However, if you dissatisfy a customer you not only risk losing their lifetime spend with you, but you risk them telling 9–13 friends of their dissatisfaction. How many of those 9–13 friends will also tell 9–13 of their friends?

The problem with unhappy customers is that often you never get to know that they were unhappy and you never get the chance to put things right. For every one customer who complains they reckon nine don't bother – they simply walk away, never come back and tell all their friends never to buy from you.

Of those who do complain, handle the complaint badly and you'll keep only 25 per cent of the customers, who'll still tell 10 people how badly you dealt with them. Handle a complaint well and you could retain 60 per cent of the customers. Handle a complaint really well and you could retain 95 per cent of the customers, plus they'll compliment you to six friends. It costs seven times as much to win back lost customers and four times as much to win new ones than it does to keep existing customers.

The moral of the story is clear – once you've got customers, give them great service or they'll leave. Loyal customers are cheaper to deal with. Encourage people to share their gripes and complaints – better you get the chance to put things right than customers walking away and you never knowing what you're doing wrong.

Warwick Business School undertook some research into the cost of service failure in the airline industry. For different problems in the areas of seat allocation, delays, baggage, food quality, cancellations, overbooking, smoking, ticketing and so forth they indicated that while a very small percentage of people actually complained, the percentage of people who used the service again fell significantly at a cost of £26.1 million in lost revenue for the airline.

DISASTER VERSUS DELIGHT EXPERIENCES

While you're thinking about any experiences you've had where the customer service (or any interaction with a human) has been a delight or a disaster, let me share some of mine with you.

I flew Virgin Atlantic from Gatwick to New York a few years ago with expectations of great service: friendly, approachable, nothing-too-much-trouble stewardesses, lots of entertainment on board, great with kids and so on. Check-in went well; really helpful staff who said they'd do what they could to make sure I was in a seat where I could do some work I needed to do. Now I know she didn't make any promises, but the last thing I expected was to have to sit next to two young kids travelling on their own. I asked a stewardess if it would be possible to move to a seat where I could work. Not a smile, not a look of sympathy – nothing, not even an explanation of why it would be difficult to move me. The reply was 'No, you can't'. Okay, I admit it – I am already wound up by her attitude. But would her being a bit more pleasant have made what was about to happen any easier to swallow?

As it happens the kids were really sweet and mannerly. But, after the initial doling out of the free kiddie packs, not once did anyone from Virgin come near them to ask if they were fine. Not once in the entire flight! I had to show them how to use the games and take them to the toilet (I stood outside only!) When it came to the meal time and the boy wondered where the special meal his dad had ordered for him was, I got him to press his call button to ask the stewardess – well – the stomp down that aisle must have dislodged so much cargo that it explained why the luggage took so long to come off. He was told not to play with the buttons, as they are 'for emergencies only'! When I explained about the pre-ordered meal I was told: 'There is no record of an order or we would have given him it!' Nice.

It will take a lot to convince me to fly Virgin again, especially where there is so much choice. Don't assume that your customers don't have choice. It says a lot about your business if you go for or rely on customers who don't have a choice.

My delight relates to Debenhams Wedding List service. The process itself is great fun – you go to the department in store and register your details. You're given a handheld scanner whereupon you go around the store zapping the barcode of any items you want on the wedding list. Back to the list department you go with your scanner and they print off your wedding list, allowing you to make manual changes there and then, and anytime thereafter. You're given vouchers for free coffee in the store to revive you after the scanning experience and offers to redeem against any other purchases or services in store. You give a preferred delivery date for any items guests wish to be delivered rather than personally presented to you. Guests simply go into the store to a touch screen and type in the bride and groom names whereupon an up-to-date list is printed out for them to purchase from. The whole service for me as bride and for guests was painless. The delivery was perfect too – they even called me the day before to check the date and time was still convenient. Every person I dealt with from the deliveryman to the office storing the list was a delight. Throughout the whole experience I was made to feel special and important.

I have raved about the service to all my bride-to-be friends. Likewise I have slated John Lewis whose service and attitude was so appalling that we decided not to have a list there at all, and M&S whose service for bride and guests was so poor that it'd take me far too long to explain! As I write this I'm wondering whether my delight with Debenhams is due really to great service, or to the fact that M&S and John Lewis were dreadful. Would I be so delighted if I had not also had a list at M&S? I suppose the moral is to ensure that your service is great in relation to competitors. Check out what your competitors are doing –where is there scope to improve on them?

I wonder if you found it easier to remember the disasters than the delights? If you did then bear it in mind – that's what your customers do. They will talk much more animatedly to others about your failings than they will your positives.

Maybe disaster experiences occur when customers have high expectations – like I did with Virgin or with M&S. Maybe my delight experience with Debenhams was as a result of having a lower expectation than what I would get from M&S. As part of your groundwork you must find out what customer expectations are and what they will accept as a minimum – then overdeliver. But never overpromise and underdeliver.

We live in a world where our expectations are ever increasing. What was seen as great service last year may no longer be acceptable or unique this year and certainly not enough to have me raving to my friends about you – but get it wrong, and boy, will I talk about you.

Customers are only prepared to put up with so much hassle before they end their relationship with you. I might have a corner shop 20 steps from my front door – such convenience may outweigh bad service in the shop, but only for so long until I take my business elsewhere – as a shopkeeper do not rely on convenience to keep your customers. Banks have relied for years on the hassle of change as being barrier to people changing their bank – just beware new companies who can take away the hassle for your customers and so remove any switching costs you relied on in the past. It is a poor company indeed that says they get business because their customers can't or can't be bothered to move elsewhere.

A piece of work I really admire was done many years ago at SAS airline company, and had such an effect on the business that many companies large and small could be encouraged to learn from it. The CEO, Jan Carlzon,[1] introduced the term 'moments of truth' as 'never to be repeated opportunities to distinguish ourselves in a memorable fashion from each and every one of our competitors'. The work was based around the knowledge that your business will only be able to develop loyalty if it satisfies customers at every *service encounter* and point of contact.

You are looking for current sources of displeasure and potential sources of delight you can offer the customer at each point of contact, and remember, it's across the *whole* customer journey. Think about a visit to your supermarket, or the 'journey' you make to take a flight. The journey for the flight covers everything from trying to book a seat through the travel agent or over the Internet, to whether the stewardess was polite, to the meal being good, reaching the destination on time and the in-flight entertainment working. The supermarket car park may be full, the traffic may be horrendous, the trolleys may be wet or with wonky wheels, the shelves may be empty and the staff may not be able to tell you which aisle Nurofen is in.

Some things you can't do anything about: a traffic jam really is not your fault, but a bad experience like this does set the customer off on the wrong foot and makes them much more sensitive to everything else they are going to experience – speaking with your reception desk, how long it takes to be seen, a dirty floor or inability to provide answers. However, a great business will anticipate how they will turn the customer round in any such eventually. Therefore you need to anticipate and identify negatives you can deal with, establish a recovery process and set standards for recovery (more on this later in the complaint handling section)

As 'moments of truth' shows, customer service is not about smiles on the phone or a smiling face behind the counter or saying, 'have a nice day'. It's about every service encounter being positive. Let's look more at what customer service is and is not: what is good and bad service?

GOOD AND BAD SERVICE DEFINED

Call it research if you like, but here are some things I was told by people on asking what bad service meant to them:

- intimidating staff
- staff chatting to each other and ignoring you
- aloof staff with airs and graces
- being pounced on by a salesperson before having time to look around
- staff with no product knowledge
- 10 staff filling forms and 1 serving
- no one to ask questions of or serve when needed
- negative and defensive starts to sentences
- having to explain your problem over and again to different people

■ passed from person to person, none of whom have authority to solve the problems or be able to help
■ staff who don't use initiative
■ company policy coming before putting things right
■ slow to help
■ never calling back when they promise they will
■ don't keep you informed
■ invoice or delivery or prices or something always wrong.

They found it easy to tell me what bad service was. What about good service?:

■ personal service, not treated like just another customer
■ genuine and natural people
■ staff who go the extra mile to put things right
■ anything that surprises and delights that you didn't expect
■ more than just good service
■ helpful and knowledgeable employees
■ enough staff to cope with busy periods
■ no quibble refund policies
■ consistent honest approach when things go wrong
■ offering solutions
■ compensation for trouble caused.

Some businesses, especially big companies, have 'formulas' in place for their approach to customer service – a central procedure for doing things a certain way, that is computerised and often very remote. Customers perceive the formula to be more about efficiency and time saving than about really giving good service. They make promises to be more efficient, to serve customers better, to make the customer's life easier and to reduce the hassle. The customer feels let down when the promises are broken, delivered half baked or not delivered at all. The customer feels remote and uncared for when they're put on hold, misinformed or when a history of being a regular and loyal customer seems to count for nothing and when there is never any follow through or contact as expected. Formula customer 'service' leaves the customer feeling ignored, inferior, dissatisfied and let down.

As a small business, don't follow this big company example. Great customer service acts can be spontaneous, but the whole attitude should not be. Providing outstanding service can differentiate you – by leaving customers feeling valued and special you create in them a sense of loyalty to your business. The following four levels of customer service I'll leave you to consider. Hopefully you can see that levels 1 and 2 are not enough in today's market where choice is everywhere. Look at levels 3 and 4 and see where you can deliver excellent and outstanding customer service. Take the opportunity to be better than large companies – it's an area that is not going to cost you anything really in the short term and could be one of your best long-term investments.

1. Indifferent – clients are not treated as individuals, company policy dominates, unskilled and untrained staff
2. Basic – polite, friendly and courteous but inconsistent
3. Excellent – clear and consistent standards, all staff work hard to deliver
4. Outstanding – amaze and delight customers, delivered with flair, confidence, and spontaneity.

What is outstanding will depend on your competitors and will depend on the expectations of your customers. This is why customer service rules are difficult – my definition of great service may not be that of another. Try to deal with people as individuals. Try to be spontaneous. Make every one of your staff committed and authorised to provide great service both before and after things go wrong.

Some examples of outstanding service

Firstly, a very simple one. My hair is quite short and grows quite quickly. Therefore it loses its style within a few weeks of being cut. My hairdresser offered, totally unprompted, to cut half as much twice as often for the same price. Great. Rather than pay £30 every six weeks for a hairstyle that looks great for three weeks only I pay

£15 every three weeks for a hairstyle that always looks great. That is outstanding service.

Here's another example that I guarantee would make potential customers think the world of you!

Let's say for arguments sake you are a provider of promotional merchandise: you know: key rings, pencils, t-shirts and so on. A customer places an order from your catalogue for some plastic figures to go into crackers they are making. As orders are being taken from your customers, the plastic figures are *en route* from your supplier. When they arrive you get ready to start posting them out to fulfil all the orders you took. Horror of horrors, compared to the items your supplier presented to you, these are pretty poor quality – a customer would certainly not be happy with the quality compared to the description of them in your catalogue. What do you do? Three choices:

■ say nothing, and send them out to customers anyhow
■ tell customers you are not able to send them the items (give an excuse or tell them the real reason)
■ tell customers you are not happy with the quality, they can have them for nothing, and hope they are prepared to wait for the new stock.

By now, everything we have been through together, please don't say that you'd choose the first option! Never lie to or cause customers to be disillusioned with what you do: 'Oh them, they had a great catalogue and great advertising and the girl on the phone who took my order was so helpful and friendly – but the products they sell are really dreadful!' is what they tell everyone. 'They think that their glossy marketing can fool me, do they think their customers are stupid?' They buy once but will they (or everyone they know) ever buy again. Remember advertising can sell a poor product – but only once.

I reckon the third option is a pretty good one, especially as you hopefully have not had to pay your supplier for items that were not as described to you. Customers will see you as honest and open and genuinely helpful. What really is the cost to you? Postage and a letter? Costs worth incurring for the chance of future business from them – especially if they are a client whom you see as being a priority one for you.

If a mistake is handled well this can cement a relationship more than error-free service from a company that shows lack of interest in its customers. It's apparent then that how you deal with the complaints of your customers is going to be key. So below are some thoughts on the area of recovering from failed service.

RECOVERING FROM FAILED
SERVICE – PUTTING THINGS RIGHT

Put your customer hat on and have a think back to a personal example of service failure of a company (or individual) you were dealing with. What attempts did they make to recover from their failings? Did they succeed in resolving the situation to your satisfaction and if so how? What steps could they have taken to recover more quickly or efficiently?

As I mentioned before, I really think that small businesses are better positioned to recover from failed service, as they don't generally have the tiresome systems and procedures or 'company policy' in place that drives the customer mad every time he or she is given it as an excuse for why they can't do anything for you.

An easy (and I know it looks a bit formal, but please bear with me) approach to handling complaints and putting things right is to go through the following four steps that are easy for you and for any member of staff to remember and act upon.

1. Response	– make sure it is speedy
	– acknowledge the problem
	– apologise for the problem
	– empathise with the customer
	– involve others who can help early.
2. Information	– explain reason for the failure (and accept responsibility)
	– get customer views on a solution
	– agree a solution
	– give assurances it won't happen again
	– written apology.

3. Action   – correct the failure internally
                     – change procedures
                     – follow up to check hasn't happened again.

4. Compensation   – a big gesture
                     – worth more to customer than you.

Of course you shouldn't ignore that there are some customers who are chronic complainers. Some companies keep a database of complainers to check the frequency and nature of their complaints. I remember one bottle of whisky being sent back to the manufacturer claiming that it tasted 'funny' and the customer wanted a refund and a replacement bottle. Of course, it had taken the customer quite some time to decide that it tasted funny – there was a tiny dribble of alcohol left in the bottle. The sample was sent for analysis and found to contain traces of exactly that – urine! On checking across the company database we found that this was not the first time the customer had done this. He didn't know that the same company owned the three other brands he'd done it to or that the same person handled the complaints. You may need to decide as a business whether you still want that person as a customer – when does the customer stop being right?

Fortunately customers who complain fraudulently are in the minority. Do not assume every person complaining is not genuine. Deal with the situation quickly and move on to delighting and retaining the real ones. What is the cost to you of a replacement bottle of whisky compared to losing the annual income generated by your other loyal customers who had a genuine complaint? When the amounts involved are small the customer is always right! If you go around trying to guess who is a liar, you are likely to get it wrong and your risk alienating a good and potentially great customer. Take a long term view – only when someone really starts to take advantage should you consider sending them elsewhere.

Customer service golden rules

■ underpromise and overdeliver
■ give employees authority to handle complaints – give them clear guidelines (that customers understand too) clear policies

such as when £ back, when free, when gift, when repair, when collect, etc.
- ask rude customers to shop elsewhere
- encourage complaints
- learn from how the best do it
- walk the talk/do what you want others to do
- mystery shop yourself to see your service levels first hand.

SUMMARY CHECKLIST

- Bad service is the main reason customers leave – much more than price
- People – you and your staff make the difference
- People will share disaster stories more than delights
- Need to know customer expectations if you are to delight
- Customer service does not mean only smiles
- Customer service means every service encounter in the whole experience of your offer being brilliant
- Have a recovery process for when things go wrong
- Making customers feel special and valued can encourage loyalty.

9

Building Customer Relationships To Encourage Loyalty

Be polite to all, but intimate with a few.
Thomas Jefferson

THE CHAPTER AT A GLANCE

We've covered the different elements of the marketing mix that go into providing a great offer and to satisfying your customers better than the competition; satisfying them so much that they won't go to the bother of looking elsewhere for alternative providers; so much that they will tell all their friends and contacts to come to you. The cost of constantly acquiring new customers is much higher than that of retaining the ones you already have. It is easier to satisfy customers you know well than it is to do so for new and prospect customers. It is expensive to repeatedly research into what new customers really want. Customer loyalty, customer retention, whatever you want to call it should be the aim of every business – staying ahead of the game means keeping your customers as loyal as possible. But loyalty must be continually earned.

Pick up any new marketing book or read any marketing article and I bet they at least mention CRM – customer relationship marketing. This is the based on the principle that you can earn loyalty by building strong relationships.

This chapter is one to think about once you're up and running and you have a great offer in place, one that you know is satisfying customers. It will help you start to think about how you could build strong relationships as a means of ensuring loyalty, and help you decide with whom it is important to build loyalty.

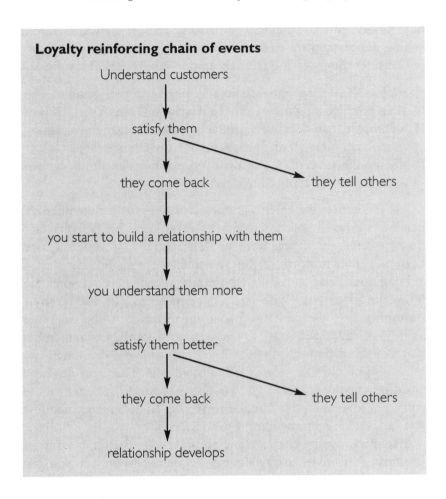

Loyalty reinforcing chain of events

Understand customers
↓
satisfy them
↓
they come back → they tell others
↓
you start to build a relationship with them
↓
you understand them more
↓
satisfy them better
↓
they come back → they tell others
↓
relationship develops

WHY IS LOYALTY SO IMPORTANT?

It takes time to develop loyalty. Just as with partners, it takes time to develop relationships with customers. If everything goes well, the chain of events above could go on and on. Without loyal customers it would be hard to build a relationship. Without a relationship it is hard to develop loyalty further.

I am not saying that loyalty and relationships exist in spite of your customer offer. Loyalty will only build a relationship if the core offer is competitive. The best relationship in the world will not retain customers of your black and white television sets if the world has moved onto all singing and dancing colour, digital, surround sound, remote control, flat screen versions.

Consider the following facts about the importance of loyalty.

■ it costs 7–10 times more to acquire new customers than to keep your existing ones (Yankee Research Group)
■ a company can double its profits by retaining just 5 per cent more customers (Bain Management Consultants)
■ the top 20 per cent of a company's customers generate, on average, 80 per cent of its profits.

Just these three statements are powerful support for the financial benefits of keeping key customers loyal. Loyalty benefits also become apparent if you were to think about how much a loyal customer is really worth to you over their life as a customer.

Imagine a loyal customer who could spend £20 per week for 50 weeks for 25 years with you. That equates to £25 000 revenue. Assuming a 10 per cent profit margin means that one customer alone is worth £2500 profit to you if they are loyal. Now remember that every satisfied customer will tell on average 3–5 friends (we must assume a loyal customer is a satisfied one). Therefore this loyal customer is actually worth £125 000 revenue and £12 500 profit to you – not to mention the knock-on effect of friends recommending you to friends recommending you to friends.

Imagine someone comes along and takes the customer away, or you force them to leave by dissatisfying them. Not only do you lose their lifetime spend and profit, but they may tell 9–13 people of the dissatisfaction. You therefore jeopardise £250 000 revenue and £25 000 profit (assume 10 friends told), not to mention the knock-on effect of friends telling friends telling friends.

There is no doubt that loyalty is important, or that a strong relationship can develop it further. Loyalty through a relationship makes it harder for competitors to lure customers away. If you take information given to you by your customers, information that has taken time and experience to compile, and you use it well, then customers may be unwilling to spend all that time again starting from scratch teaching the new supplier everything you already know. This is called a switching cost – having a great relationship with a customer is an example of a switching cost – it costs the customer too much (not necessarily financial) to change supplier. Switching costs are great barriers to entry to have in your business.

ESTABLISHING RELATIONSHIPS

The drive behind developing relationships with customers as a route to loyalty comes not only from businesses looking for a way to stay ahead of the game, but also from customers themselves. In some markets there is so much choice available that customers are keener to develop deeper relationships with a smaller number of trusted businesses and brands. Relationships will thrive where there is mutual value: where there is benefit for the business and the customer.

The CRM principles say that you should be looking to develop one-to-one marketing. Mutual gain comes from you knowing so much about one individual and dealing with them in such a tailored manner that you provide value, and in return get their loyalty.

As one-to-one relationships may be impossible with every single customer you have you should identify the 20 per cent of customers who provide 80 per cent of your business. This 80 : 20 generalisation is usually true in most markets and businesses. It is these key 20 per cent of your customers on whom you really need to focus your attempts to develop a relationship. So once your business is rolling the first thing you need to do is to identify your key customers.

The second thing you need to do is to get to know them: their behaviour, expectations, needs and preferences. You've done much of this already in the process of choosing your target markets and understanding the real needs you are satisfying. But this is looking in even more depth, individually if possible, at your key 20 per cent.

Years ago the corner shop owner knew all of his customers. He knew what they liked and didn't like. He knew that Mrs Allen bought unsmoked streaky bacon while Mrs Baxter liked smoked lean back. Building relationships was easier – he knew them so well that he knew how to satisfy them. It was easy for him to generate sales for new products. When he got a new line of pickles in his store he knew exactly who to sell them to – Mrs Thomson who already was a pickle buyer and Mrs Russell who bought cold meats and bread for sandwich making.

A small restaurant is great at relationship building where the waiter knows your name, remembers your favourite seat, reminds you which wine you enjoyed last time – in general he recognises your repeat business.

With hundreds even thousands of customers, it's hard for big companies in particular to try to replicate this sort of relationship. Hence the role of databases in replacing the individual memory. British Airways' database tries to replicate a personal relationship with its Executive Club members by recognising the seat and meal preferences of individuals on presentation of their membership number. However, databases are not people – the accuracy of the database could be questionable.

SEVEN STEPS TO BUILDING RELATIONSHIPS FOR LOYALTY

One to one marketing has been spoken about since Don Peppers and Martha Rogers wrote *The One-to-One Future* back in 1993.[1] Here we are years later and still not many companies are really 'doing' one-to-one. I think that the opportunities to do so are much better for the small company than the large – so take advantage of this. You have the potential to be much closer to your customers than they will ever be. Peppers and Rogers say there are seven steps to one-to-one marketing:

Remember your customer

Know who they are. We have only just covered the introduction to this section, and already we have identified this one reason why you will be better than huge corporations with millions of customers worldwide. Even with the most sophisticated database and computer systems and the loyalty cards they use to gather information about their customers, they will never really know and remember details of all of them. Having a database and remembering people are two entirely different things. How many times have you checked into the same hotel chain, or booked a table at a large restaurant chain or telephoned financial companies to request quotes for insurance and so forth, and you find yourself having to give them a repeat of the information you gave them every other time – name, address and so on?

How do you think it makes the customer react? 'They have no idea who I am nor am I important to them at all, they never remember me despite the fact I am a regular here.' Having a waiter in a restaurant remember your name, a barman remember your favourite drink, a hotel remember where you live and that you like a non-smoking room and *The Times* rather than the *Guardian* are little things that go a long way to delivering superior value to customers.

Remember customers across all you do for them

Your receptionist in the hotel may know and remember your customers, but do the bar staff, the waiting staff in the restaurant? Will their ignorance ruin all the great relationship building work done by the receptionist?

Imagine the huge financial services company or bank that you may have your current account, loans, savings, investments and credit cards through. One part of the bank may be really good at servicing your current account and have a great direct mail campaign targeting current account users. Yet the credit card division may treat you as though you hardly exist, and may never increase your credit level despite the fact that your salary has risen 30 per cent in the last three years, something that their own current account division should notice. Does their pensions division continue to send you information about a pension assuming you do not yet have one – despite the fact that the current account shows you make monthly contributions to a pension provider? Big banks are still struggling to get their separate product-focused (instead of customer-focused) databases and divisions to talk to each other so that they understand and get a complete picture of the customer. The customer does not care that the problem was due to a different division of the company – the problem was the company full stop! This again is why smaller companies are at an advantage over larger ones.

If you are a small financial services company you probably have your records organised by customer rather than by product. You are in a much better position to have the complete picture.

Do something with the information

Do not take the information you have for granted – use it actively. Again as a small company you are in a good position to look at all the information you have about a client, build up a picture about their past and potential future requirements, take a view on how much they are worth to you, and plan what you will do for them as individuals. Do the records show that until last month they bought from you every Friday for the last three years? Find out why this is the case. Have you had a new line of pickles into your natural food store and you want to target customers to try them? Look to see (because of the first two steps above you will be able to) who buys products that complement pickles, or other pickles you sell and focus on them initially – much better than trying to take a broad approach for everyone. Remember the big competitors have lots of information about their customers from the loyalty cards (name, address, how much you spend on an average visit, how often you visit, how loyal you are to brands, which brands you prefer, do you have children, do price cuts influence you, or do you buy more with other promotional offers). But they are only now getting expert at using this information effectively. It takes them time to track the behaviour of their customers through their computer systems, and then more time to identify who buys pickles or hams, and then more time to prepare a mail shot or coupon to send to those customers, who may not plan another supermarket trip until next week. By the time that customer (who may not even read the direct mail coupon, but throw it straight in the bin) gets to the store, your small business has already delivered superior value to your customers.

Interact properly with customers

This means capturing each in-coming customer contact – whether a phone call, a letter, face-to-face contact, a complaint or a website enquiry – and linking them to see the relationship as the customer sees it, a seamless entity. Simon has placed an order with you, to be delivered to his home next Tuesday. The order taker inputs the details. On Monday Simon is called away and will not be at home to collect the delivery, so he calls and asks if it can be delivered to an alternative address. Make sure you keep a record of that alternative address. Next time Simon places an order give him the option of either address to deliver to – show him you remember and that no matter who he speaks to in your company the relevant information is held. If Jan telephones or e-mails or writes to let you know of a change of address make sure that every area of your company knows and that all records are amended. Ask her, next time you speak, if she has settled into and is enjoying her new home. If she had a query about holiday locations to which she could take pets, log it, and make sure everyone knows this is of importance and could be relevant in the future. If a gym member makes a complaint about a class teacher not turning up, or about double-parking blocking them in the car park, or an error in the timing of a programme session resulting in a rushed reprogramme, then log it, capture it. Make sure that that contact is never lost, make sure that your staff know to apologise for it next time the member visits the gym, make sure next time a programme is booked that they get a longer session – all things that make the customer see you as a super-efficient machine. Having information about customers that competitors don't have lets you compete on things they don't even know about.

Customise communication with them

One-to-one success means becoming what Peppers and Rogers call the customer's 'trusted agent'. Customisation of communications, core products and services have to take place so that customers feel special. Never ever make the customer feel as though they are just one of hundreds of people whom this standard letter has been mailed out to. All they feel is angry that they spent so long giving information about themselves that has been ignored when it could have been really useful.

I got married last year and helped my mother go through the painful 'mother-of-the-bride-outfit' search. I remember being very impressed by one store in Glasgow who remembered my mum had visited several months earlier (oh yes, the process took months). They had taken her contact details that first day and promised to call if anything they felt to be suitable came into stock. True to their word they called to ask whether she had anything yet and told her about new stock just in. They didn't send a standard mail shot, they remembered her tastes – and while my mum didn't go on to buy anything she has been back since and she has shared her positive experience with others.

When someone complains that the exercise class they used to enjoy is too crowded and writes to you asking if you would consider adding another class each week, please do not send them a standard letter saying: 'We know how much you love the class, we're glad you're still attending and want to let you know that the time of the class is changing from 7 pm to 8 pm'.

Encourage information sharing

The sign of a great relationship is where customers are willing to share more information with the supplier over time, because the supplier uses that additional data to good effect – the supplier gives benefits to the customer. Only at this stage do customers become 'locked-in' to the relationship, partly because they have invested so much in it and partly because it has become valuable to them. My local wine bar has locked me into a relationship by being expert at recognising which wines I like, always having them in stock, and by suggesting wines they know I'll also like based on my current tastes.

Keep it all going

Now the really hard bit! Make sure you don't irritate customers who have evolved from one stage in their life to another. Mary may be on your database as a mother, but that does not excuse you seven years later still sending her mails about offers on nappies. Keep up to date. Building relationships and maximising customer value take time, so please do not sacrifice them for the sake of short-term sales results when desperate. If you let a customer down or disappoint him, it will be a struggle to convince him back, and harder to get him to share information with you.

SOME EXAMPLES

Here are some examples of the above in practice – and some examples of how some companies could do much more than they are.

Hallmark Cards and American Greetings have installed electronic kiosks in stores and other public places to enable people to create their own greeting cards.[2] After browsing through selections and wordings for varieties of cards, their personal choice is printed in a minute or so. But how could the companies improve on this? The biggest weakness of the system is the absence of recording individual customers' preferences. Each time a customer uses the system they must start from the beginning. So how about if the system could remember important occasions and remind you to buy a card? It could make suggestions based on your past purchases. The kiosk could show previous purchases you have made to ensure you don't send the same card more than once to the same person.

Not every customer wants a relationship like this, perhaps they can't be bothered to invest the time telling the company about themselves, or perhaps ethically they may think it not right to let a company know so much – 'What does Big Brother really do with this information?' Likewise, maybe you have some customers who buy so infrequently from you, and who you see as having little potential to turn into higher worth customers, that you don't want to spend too much time building anything other than an acceptable relationship with them. This is all about mutual value.

Getting information is easy if you are a hotel, restaurant or any such business where you have direct contact with customers – their names, transactions and preferences are easy to track. But if you sell through retailers or wholesalers and don't have that direct contact, you need to encourage the customers.

For example, Waldenbooks[3] offers a 10 per cent discount on all purchases to customers who identify themselves by joining their Preferred Readers scheme. The programme allows the company to track purchases. This allows the bookseller to let a particular customer know when the next novel by the author they like comes in, or when an author whose work the customer has purchased will be in a local store signing books. Their scheme is aimed at people who spend more than $100 per year on their books. As a screening device, they charge an annual fee for Preferred Reader status.

Maybe it is best to begin with your best and most valuable customers and gradually expand the programme to others.

We mentioned how important it is to 'remember the customer'. This means remembering everything, not just past purchases, but also preferences that emerge from questions, complaints, suggestions and actions. The Ritz Carlton hotel chain trains its entire staff – from front desk to maintenance and housekeeping – how to converse with customers and how to handle complaints immediately. But better than that, they provide all staff with a 'guest preference pad' for writing down every preference gleaned from every conversation and observation. Every day these preferences are entered into the nationwide database of almost half a million customers. Employees at any of the worldwide Ritz Carlton hotels can access the database of profiles. If you were to stay in the hotel in Mexico, call room service for dinner and request an ice cube in your glass of white wine, when you stay in Italy and order a glass of white wine you will be asked if you'd like an ice cube in it. They also hold such information as a request for a no smoking room, window-seats in the restaurant, decaffeinated coffee or a shower rather than bath.

It is not enough to remember the customer as they were. You must keep up with their changing needs and preferences.

There is a company in the USA called Peapod,[4] a grocery shopping and delivery service. Peapod customers order their groceries online, paying a monthly service charge and an order charge; Peapod buys the groceries from supermarkets and delivers to the homes within a 90-minute time slot. Peapod software uses technology to change the shopping experience. It lets each customer create his or her personal virtual supermarket. Customers can request items by category (pet care), by item (cat food), by brand (Whiskas) or by what is on offer in-store that day. You can have the items arranged alphabetically by brand, by pack size, by unit price or even by nutritional value. Customers can create and save for repeated use standard and special shopping lists. At the end of each shopping session Peapod asks the customer how they did on the last order. They get feedback on 35 per cent of orders (most people are pleased to get 10 per cent response). The feedback has led to several changes being implemented including providing additional nutritional information, making deliveries within a 30-minute time slot for a small charge, and accepting detailed requests (such as three ripe and three unripe tomatoes). They also see the delivery process as an opportunity to find out about the customer. It asks the delivery people to find out where the customers would like the groceries left when they are not at home, and anything else that will improve the service. The four-year-old service in 1995 had 7500 customers, revenues of about $15 million, a customer retention rate of more than 80 per cent, and accounted for almost 15 per cent of the sales of the supermarkets where Peapod shops for its customers.

SUMMARY CHECKLIST

- Retaining loyal customers should be the aim of your business – but loyalty must be earned
- Loyalty builds relationships which can themselves build loyalty
- Loyalty is key among the 20 per cent of your customers who account for 80 per cent of your business
- Relationships can be switching costs, protecting you from the competition
- Make the relationship as one-to-one as possible in order to gain mutual value
- Remember customers across everything you do for them – not just the last contact you had

- Interact properly with customers using all the information you know
- Customise your approach to them
- Remember as a small business you are closer to the customer than a large business can be, so building relationships should be simpler.

10

Using the Web/Internet

Do you Yahoo?

THE CHAPTER AT A GLANCE

In April 2000, MMXI Europe research announced that 9.6 million of the 60 million people living in the UK 'used' the Internet. ('Used' meaning went online in the last four weeks, so it's a pretty up-to-date figure of active users.) That figure is a huge jump from the 7.8 million active users only four months previously. And compared to countries like Sweden and USA where online customers account for 45 per cent and 37 per cent of the population respectively, the potential for growth in the UK is still huge. It is reckoned that 700 million people worldwide use the Internet, and that over 50 per cent of businesses are online. In terms of users adopting the technology, it has achieved in five years what it took radio 30 years to reach.

Yet despite continued growth of use of the Internet, every week seems to bring news of another failure, more millions lost, more Internet millionaires losing everything. Pure Internet companies and more established businesses and brands incorporating it into their business strategy are finding it hard to make it work well for them.

This chapter therefore looks at how to make the Internet work well for you – whether you are an Internet business or whether you are a business using the Internet to support the other parts of your business.

THE ROLE OF THE INTERNET
IN YOUR MARKETING MIX OFFER

The Internet, World Wide Web whatever you want to call it, has become and probably will feature as one of the key elements of your marketing mix. Whether you see the Web as part of the communications mix to speak to and hear from customers, or whether part of the distribution mix for selling to customers, there's a lot to consider. Is your site user friendly, is it search friendly, does it take forever to download, is your payment system in place?

When you get it right the Internet is an information resource for both you and your customers. You can build a database and gather information from your users, and customers can see the quality and operation of your business. Therefore it is vital that you integrate your Internet presence into your whole marketing strategy – make it consistent with your image, your offers, your communication and so on. Your presence on the Internet could be as simple or as sophisticated as you wish and will depend on your objectives. The different levels of presence you may go for are shown opposite. One of the places to go which I recommend, particularly for help in developing an Internet strategy is clearlybusiness.com – a new venture in association with Barclays and Freeserve. They give very clear guidelines in using the Internet for any of the three levels of presence you require. It is full of valuable information such as:

Business homepage	– include name and business logo
	– brief description of what you do
	– summary of your services
	– address and contact information
	– visuals to demonstrate your offer
	– request feedback on the page
	– track its success, when you get a new lead come through, ask if it came as a result of your homepage.
Business website	– should be as easy to flick through as a physical printed brochure
	– ensure it is always up to date.

E-commerce   – fully understand the statutory rights of customers
– refunds policies must be compliant with the Consumer Credit Act 2000 (Distance Selling).

Many big branded companies have, through painful and expensive experience, learned that brand-based sites do not work. Mars.com, Dolmio.com, Evian.com, for example, failed. People have no time nor are they really interested in plugging into sites such as these – what are they going to find out that really interests them?

Companies are increasingly developing sites that are driven by needs that customers have, for example I may not be interested in washing powder or liquid or laundry, but on Saturday morning when I spot that the dress I want to wear out on my date that night has stains on it, I desperately want to know how best to get those stains out. An Ariel website therefore might have a site where I can tap in the problem with my garment and in return get suggestions on how to clean it quickly at home. Similarly I may not be interested in going into Oil-of-Olay.com, but what I am interested in is how to slow down the onset of laughter lines around my eyes (oh all right then, wrinkles).

What the Internet can provide therefore is an opportunity for your products and services to go beyond conventional offerings – to offer information yes, but also solutions and benefits to problems

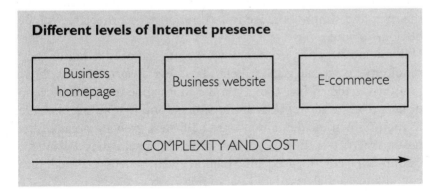

Different levels of Internet presence

| Business homepage | Business website | E-commerce |

COMPLEXITY AND COST

customers have. Your homepage could be the information provider, a business website must be based on clear benefits to customers, and e-commerce could provide for sale the solutions you are offering to customer problems or needs. Whatever the level, just remember the concept of marketing – the site must be an experience the customer enjoys (if they can find it and wait long enough to enter it!). It must be important enough for people to bother going to.

So here are some basic tips and ideas for the design and operation of your site in whichever capacity you are using it.

BASIC TIPS AND IDEAS ON DESIGN AND OPERATION OF YOUR SITE

Before I move onto some specifics regarding a site on the Internet, one of my main tips is to make it adaptable – it is easier to add bits to it as you grow than to go back to the drawing board because your initial idea isn't working and isn't adaptable enough to amend.

Site design and image need to be right

Firstly, I'd say make sure that the design of your site reflects the products or service you are offering, the customers you are targeting and the image you want to convey as a business in everything you do. Having read previous chapters on consistency in all elements of the mix, and simply because it is common sense, then this will be obvious to you!

If you are targeting teenage boys, the site will need to match their requirements, teenage girls theirs, business investors theirs, busy housewives theirs. Just take a minute to imagine the differences in design of a site selling skincare to women and that selling skincare to men (which incidentally is one the fastest growing areas of the beauty market in Europe). How different would they be in, for example, the colours used, information given, benefits claimed, sites you link to, models used and packaging shown?

A site will have a marketing mix all of its own. You could even have a different website name suitable for each target market in order to lead them to your site. Try not to think of site design as merely putting down everything your company brochure shows. Think about how the commercial website can project the same image as customers would get from direct contact with you.

Do you want to be funky and fun or professional and serious? Are you quirky and fast moving or solid and dependable? Are you big and national or local and family-run? Whatever sort of company you set out to be, whatever image you wish to portray just make sure your website supports and reinforces this positioning.

Who you are and what you are offering should be obvious

The temptation with all this technology that the Web brings is to be too clever. I'm not for one second saying customers are stupid – but to confuse is to annoy. Make it immediately clear who you are, where you are and what your product or service is. Does someone really want to click through four pages of beautiful graphics before they stumble across what you actually do? Will they even bother to keep on clicking if it is not immediately obvious? By all means capitalise on the wonders of the technology, but not at the sacrifice of communicating simply and clearly what you can actually provide people.

So, ensure your homepage makes it clear who or what you are and where people can contact you – by phone or mail as well as e-mail. This gives your potential customers the confidence to buy from you by proving you are a 'real' entity and not some here today gone tomorrow virtual body behind the Web.

If I am looking for a landscape gardener, I'd like to know up-front the extent of the work they do: Do they design, install and maintain the work? Do they work only in one region? Do they work for business or residential customers? Do they only work in the Japanese minimalist style?

If you are a management training company, make it clear which skills you train in – marketing, finance, people skills, IT, operational skills? Do you run tailored courses or open programmes? As the owner of a small business looking for some training for my staff I would find it pretty helpful to know immediately whether you are the right company to consider for training my two office staff in PowerPoint skills.

To make it as clear as possible what you are offering, try to avoid using business or industry specific jargon. 'We are a complete T&D provider, working through the value chain from TNA to post learning embedding' might sound grand and be perfectly in line with the professional image you wish to purvey, but honestly, does it make it clear to many non-human resources or training professionals what your scope is? 'We provide training designed specifically for your company. We are a complete provider of training and development needs – everything from identifying the needs of training in your company to ensuring people take the learning from a course back to work and start using it', may be actually what you mean.

Make entering and navigating the site easy

Make it as easy as possible for people to navigate around your site – have an index and search facility. Frustrated clicking is guaranteed to make someone switch to another site.

If you have followed the advice of the previous tip, the first thing someone views on entering your site should be clear. If you insist on doing this in a very clever and hi-tech manner, such as a slow teasing reveal, please consider your returning users: people who have seen the introduction before, people who know all the background. Are you making them suffer your creative wizardry time and again? They probably just want to get in there and see what they came for. You must give them an option at start-up to bypass the creative introductions.

Similarly, don't put up barriers that discourage people from entering your site. What do I mean? If someone has to register by giving their name and address and telephone number when all they want to do is browse round, they probably won't bother. Make it as easy for someone to browse on your site as it is for him or her to browse in a high street shop. You may say that if someone is prepared to register, they must be serious and not a time waster, but who are you to decide? Don't lose the opportunity to convert browsers to buyers or turn off serious customers who can't be bothered registering.

There is, of course, a very real advantage if you can get customers to register and sign in when coming to your site – you can track their visits, monitor their interest, and respond with personalised e-mails and pages. But do this in addition to having standard pages for people to look at. Let these standard introductory pages explain the benefits of your offer and of registering. Give them a reason to register. Don't let registering in order to even know who you are and what you do be the reason potential customers click away.

Reflect.com is a custom beauty products site that makes visitors fill out a multiscreen registration before they can even see a product, let alone shop. Before you even see a product you could buy, you have to fill out a lengthy and cynicism enhancing questionnaire that asks you to choose: 'If you were a house, what kind of house would you be?' As the questioning continues you start to question your own rationale for being here, and all along you are thinking *how* is this related to make-up? Don't rely on this intrigue keeping customers – I left before I'd even caught a whiff of anything remotely beautifying.

If you are going to use pictures or illustrations as icons for clicking into subpages then, unless the pictures are blindingly obvious, have explanation tabs that come up when the cursor is placed over them. If you are going to offer links to other sites, make sure it is easy to get back to your pages from them.

A good way to explain this is to imagine your webpage as if it were a shop someone was coming into. You want people to like the look of the shop enough to browse around, or if they know what they want to buy then easy enough for them to get there to find the items. You probably want your stock merchandised in easy to shop categories – the pet food and pet care items will all be stocked together, likewise the fruit and vegetables. The signs in the shop or the person behind the counter can easily direct customers to the products they are looking for. Information about the products is close to hand (on the labels or on cards beneath the products you sometimes see in wine shops or by asking a question of the staff). You can quickly find out if the products are in stock and able to be delivered soon, and you'll immediately know what the company policy on return of goods or delivery times is. If you have a large showroom you want to make sure people find their way around easily and have access to tills as they need them or near the exit just before they leave. If you're in Ikea and in going around the showroom section want to miss out bedrooms and go to kitchens, the store does not make you exit and enter again at the start, so why should a website? So think logically. Part of the attraction of the website is meant to be ease – you must make it as easily navigable as possible because people will not hang around figuring out where to go next.

How long does your site take to download?

This section is going to make customers sound even more impatient than the previous one did, but it's true! Expectations, especially of the Internet are of speed and immediacy. People generally do not wish their hair to grow an inch while waiting for a site to download. The site should be designed for 'users'.

Much as great graphics and special effects have impact, they only have impact on people who hang around long enough for your pages to download. If your page and pages do not download quickly then they will be off and away to look at another site. A recent report from Zona Research identified a factor known as the eight-second rule. If a site takes more than eight seconds to download, half of the consumers visiting the site will immediately leave. And of that half, only a quarter will ever come back. The point of business on the Web is no different to that of traditional businesses, to make customers loyal – site performance is everything to today's demanding online consumer, so make sure your site meets the high standards of the eight-second user. Don't use heavy complicated graphics.

Likewise beware very recent technology that requires a recent browser or plug-in. Many Web users won't try to download plug ins or more recent browsers which allow them to access certain visuals you have.

Is your site interactive?

Try to make your site as two-way as possible. By this we mean don't just talk to your customers, but encourage them to talk back to you. You will get helpful feedback, prompts for one-to-one communication at a later date, and good information to gather a database about potential customers.

If you are selling or showing gift items on your website, you could add to the interactivity of your site by allowing the user to enter the type of person she is buying for, the budget they have to spend, the broad type of gift they are considering.

If you are a landscape gardener, your site could ask the user to input the measurements and shape of their garden and their preferred style of garden in order to see some suggested layouts you could offer.

Anything that keeps people involved, holds their interest, makes them want to ask and search more and makes them feel that the site is for them and really understands their needs is likely to be more successful than one that doesn't.

Amazon aim to be 'the right store for you as an individual'. Jeff Bezos said that if he has 6.2 million customers then they should have 6.2 million stores. They can tailor the site to each customer (relationship marketing) by suggesting books and products similar to others they've bought.

Responding to e-mails and enquiries

If you offer the chance for people to e-mail you with queries, at least have the courtesy to answer, even if it is to say no! If people have gone to the trouble of ordering on your Web page, make sure you keep them up to date with the status of their order. Send them an e-mail confirming receipt of their order and thanking them. E-mail to tell them their goods will be despatched by X date. With so much concern about the security of ordering and giving credit card information over the Web, it goes part of the way to alleviating worry if you can speak to people to reassure them.

Make your replies as tailored as you can – it makes your site of much more value to customers. The more you are solving individual problems, satisfying individual needs you are starting to build a rapport with that user. Big companies kill for this sort of relationship building stuff. They love the Internet if they can use it to speak to customers. Remember, as a small company who can more easily develop knowledge of and relationships with customers (because you are closer to them) make sure you use the Internet to do the same. Don't hide behind the technology and become large and distant like the big companies or you take a step towards losing a big source of competitive advantage – so see the people behind the Web, use information you know about them, speak to them personally and across the Web in as knowledgeable and tailored a fashion as you can.

Amazon has 20 per cent of their staff doing nothing but answering queries from the e-mail centre. They know the dangers of hiding behind technology – they ensure humans can take over and give the personal touch when needed.

Every now and again take the opportunity to speak personally, by this I mean verbally, to your customers too. Telephone them to tell them when the order will be delivered. Call them after delivery and ask if they are happy with the items. As well as being excellent customer service, it may just protect against fraud by ensuring orders are genuine. Several companies have publicly declared sales increases when staff began following up e-mail by telephone correspondence. It seems to be so important to try to incorporate human interaction into your e-commerce – remember to many people this website stuff is a bit confusing, a bit too high tech for their liking.

What if things go wrong?

Telephone support is essential – even if customers are relatively Web literate there may come a time when they want to speak to someone on the phone to ask questions or complain or get help. Make sure you have people, enough of them, skilled enough to handle this – be especially vigilant if you are dealing internationally and need to speak languages to communicate effectively.

Keep your site up to date

There is nothing (well almost nothing) more annoying than an out-of-date website. If you have ceased updating articles, at least say on your site when the article was last updated.

One of the largest challenges and costs for many information-based websites (news, holiday, legal) is to ensure everything is kept up to date. It is the whole foundation on which their offer is based, so for it to fall at this hurdle is criminal. Imagine you are a Web-based company specialising in selling last minute holidays, tables in restaurants, theatre tickets, etc. What does it do to the credibility of your offer, never mind the sheer frustration and inconvenience for the customer if the offers are all last week's, or the offers still on the notice board today are completely sold out?

So keep your information, all of it, up to date. If you are selling anchors and outboard motors for small boats and haven't had a certain model in stock for weeks and are unlikely to for another few, let people know as easily and early as possible. Be honest with them – this model is out of stock but will be available again week commencing 23rd August. It is the same lesson Argos learnt from their catalogue stores. Customers trawl through the catalogue, get to page 1073 eventually, locate the item number they must insert on the order form, take the order form to a till point to pay. Only at the till might they be told that the item is out of stock. So, home you go or back to the catalogue, back to page 1073 to find a similar item and repeat the process. What a revelation that customers got annoyed not knowing if things were in stock. How practical and fun it is now to enter the item number into a mini terminal next to the catalogue to immediately be told if the item you want is in stock.

Can surfers and potential customers find you?

I read somewhere that there are more pages on the Web than people in the world – so imagine how difficult and therefore important it is to reach potential customers. And what if these people do not know your address (your Unique Resource Locator or URL using Web language).

You know that users will make a search on the problem/query they have, and you want to make sure that they are informed of and directed to your page – thus the importance of the search engine you use. A search engine is basically something that will canvas business on your behalf when a potential user types in a request for information on sites relating to your offers. Gaining a good position on a search engine will ensure more people visit your site.

It is worth noting that even the best search engines are only cataloguing about 16 per cent of the pages on the Web. The worst of them only canvass 2.5 per cent. So how best to ensure customers reach your products or services you offer over the Web? Well searching by key words is fine if the name of your address is directly and obviously related to the products and services you offer – e.g. Gilchrist Tropical Plants. But what if a user types in palm trees? Now your website may have a page on palm trees, but it is unlikely that the search engine will know this. What you need to ensure is that each page in your website has its own address URL, that way the search engine has access to each individual page and can flag it to the user.

Use of search engines is such a huge topic. You could do worse than read Angus Kennedy's *The Internet Rough Guide*[1] or check out www.webpromote.com

How do you handle
payment transactions and security?

There is a general expectation among users that when buying goods on the Internet, they will be able to use credit cards to do so. For small transactions credit cards can be very expensive for you the seller, because of the high commission charged. So you may only be prepared to accept cheque payments. Make sure you clearly display this policy to users right up-front before they start browsing your site and before they have gone through the entire ordering process. To some, writing and posting a cheque is a hassle, like going looking around shops, which they hate doing, which is why they use the Internet.

One of the main concerns of buying over the Web is that of security – even if exaggerated, in the customers' eyes these concerns are real and you must address them. There are specialist companies that exist to deal with aspects of e-payment and e-security: they ensure credit card numbers and transaction details remain secure.

Recently savers were warned not to open an account with First-e, the Internet bank, after security breaches and a string of complaints. The bank attracted many customers by paying an attractive, above average interest rate. But there have been many complaints about service, and they recently admitted giving one customer access to another saver's account details. Appalled, the customer withdrew her money immediately. The bank has since blamed human error, looked into how it happened, changed its systems and aims to make sure it never happens again – well they certainly won't get the opportunity with that customer again.

These problems follow others at Egg (the Prudential's Internet banking arm) and Halifax. At Egg a security breach allowed a user to get into another customer's account, and a software error at the Halifax gave its Internet share dealing customers access to other people's accounts.

DOING YOUR RESEARCH

Before you decide to make use of the wonders of the World Wide Web please make sure you have done your homework.

Consider distribution of your goods to customers – which areas of the country and world are you going to get orders from, how much will it cost you, how much of the cost will customers pay, what do you do if no one is at home to collect the items, how will you handle perishable or fragile goods?

Did you read about the enterprising Scottish salmon farmer who decided to advertise smoked Scottish salmon for sale on his tiny website? He anticipated a few orders from mainly the UK and perhaps Europe. One of the largest markets for smoked salmon is the Middle East. Having never considered the cost and the packaging problems involved in shipping salmon to hot countries, he started receiving orders from there. Fortunately he embraced a marketing principle we have mentioned several times already – he immediately and honestly e-mailed the potential clients to explain his problem, and promised to come straight back to them when he had got the distribution sorted out.

Just because we are talking about the Internet, do not forget that normal marketing principles apply. The Internet offer must satisfy customer requirements, profitably. Remember that some customers may want to be able to do business with you by whatever means suit them best. They may want to look at the products in a catalogue or in a store, before ordering they may then want to check availability by phone or Internet, they may want the items delivered to their home, and they may want to return them to a shop if they're not happy with them. One of the main reasons that online retailers fail is that, especially for clothing, beauty or furnishing items, people want to look, feel, smell and touch before buying – if you have no physical store where someone can do this before then going home to order over the Internet (maybe the shop was too busy), then you lose converting an interested party into a buyer. Maybe Internet retailing works best for repeat orders where the item has been successfully and satisfactorily used at home in the past.

Just make sure you live up to your promises in everything you do! Jeff Bezos, the founder of Amazon, knows that being online does not mean less service – it means more. Technology literate users can send one message of complaint and disappointment of bad service to over 6000 names if they so wish.

Get good help and advice if setting up any Web pages or e-commerce sites. Ask friends to recommend providers they have successfully dealt with. Go to your local chamber of commerce, and ask for the names of any small local companies who have set themselves up in the Web design business.

For help on anything to do with e-commerce UK Online for Business (0845 715 2000) www.ukonlineforbusiness.gov.uk are a good contact to have, and www.tradeuk.com is a Department of Trade and Industry site which is full of advice for anyone looking at international e-business who may have currency concerns.

SUMMARY CHECKLIST

- Make sure your site offers benefits to customers – why is it of value?
- Make your site easy to find and easy to use
- Make it clear who you are, what you do, where you are and how to contact by mail or phone
- Incorporate a human element wherever possible
- Use comments sent to you as the basis of personalised communication back to users.

11

How to Present Your Ideas

How can I hear what you are saying
when what you are is ringing in my ears?
Anon

THE CHAPTER AT A GLANCE

Have you ever felt that you had great news, great ideas, great suggestions, but no one you spoke to seemed to be as excited by them as you? You failed to get your message across. The problem was probably not the message itself but the manner in which it was delivered. Successful presentations depend very much on communicating with and influencing your audience effectively.

I thought it useful to include this as a chapter, particularly as in your role you may find yourself having to make many presentations: to banks, to prospect customers, to distributors, to staff, to your financial backers, to small business networks or to suppliers. You may be presenting to the bank to try to get money or an extension on your overdraft, you may be trying to sell your product or service to new clients, you may be trying to get a new distributor to stock your products, you may be trying to sell new ideas to staff or colleagues, you may be updating financial backers on the current business position and your future plans, you may be presenting ideas to other small businesses in your region or your staff requirements to recruitment companies or your training requirements to training suppliers.

For whatever reason, it is always helpful to have the skill of being an effective presenter of a powerful presentation, be it formal or informal, to 2 people or to 200 people. This chapter is designed to help you to do this successfully.

WHAT MAKES A SUCCESSFUL PRESENTER AND PRESENTATION?

Who might you need to present to? Here are some, but you can make your own list:

- banks
- small business networks
- prospects and customers
- suppliers
- distributors
- staff
- financial backers.

You just can't not communicate with people. Simply being around causes them to make judgements. Your manner: looking a certain way, wearing certain clothes, how confident you look, communicates something about you that others will perceive – whether true or not. This is such an important point to consider when preparing to present effectively to any of the people we have listed. Listeners will judge you and your message in roughly the following proportions:

- **What** you say 7%
- **How** you say it 38%
- How you **look** 55%.

So, you can have the strongest message matter (on paper and in your mind), but a successful presentation will depend around 90 per cent on the manner in which it is presented.

To reinforce these statistics, have a think about some of the best presentations you have seen or heard, either personally or on television or even radio (where the speaker doesn't have the 55 per cent 'how you look' factor that determines effectiveness of the message). Take a few moments to jot down the reasons why you think they were great presentations.

What did you list? Perhaps some of the following:

■ easy to follow logic and flow
■ examples to make it real
■ grabbed and held attention
■ positive attitude, energy and enthusiasm – presence
■ clever use of voice
■ confident looking and sounding
■ charts, drawings, slides to reinforce key messages
■ entertaining or informative or persuasive
■ appealed to your emotion.

Obviously, depending on the situation some may not apply, but generally you can see that these points tend to fall into the what they said, how they said it, how they looked categories.

If you ever watch MTV music channel then it's a great reminder of the performance of the artist and the staging of the video being much more likely to result in a hit record than simply the song itself – sad I know, but unfortunately true, and so important to remember in influencing your audience effectively.

Chapter 12 (How to motivate people around you) can be read in conjunction with this one – what else should a presentation do but motivate people to act? One section in that chapter focuses on the different motivational needs of individuals and the need therefore to communicate in a different manner with them. An effective presenter will ensure he or she adapts the message and the manner according to the audience. For example, if I were presenting to my bank I would be analytical, detailed, logical, specific and rational. However, presenting to people with whom I work would allow me to offer much less analysis paralysis, much more emotion, less specific detail and much more theatre. The requirements in presenting to a doctor would be totally different from presenting to a student. Therefore you should read this and the subsequent chapter with this in mind.

To help you be a great presenter and deliver great presentations the remainder of this chapter considers the following areas: purpose/objective, content/structure, delivery, and supporting material/visuals

PURPOSE/OBJECTIVE

Before even putting pen to paper or gathering your thoughts together, I urge you to clarify first and foremost the purpose of the presentation. What is your objective? It could be to inform, or persuade, or entertain, or a combination of all three things.

To inform

Perhaps you need to inform your bank or business angel of how the business has been doing, or your employees how the business is performing, or the business of new legislation that is being introduced or about a new policy or process. The danger of a presentation designed to inform is that it ends up boring the audience. Data upon data, fact after fact, chart after chart – but the human brain only has an average attention span of around 30 minutes, after which new facts become a blur. So if you aim to inform your audience beware boredom. The rational presentation of sales figures is important, but will probably have more impact if you approach it emotionally by emphasising the effect of the figures on the staff.

To persuade

Your objective may be to persuade your audience. Perhaps you are informing them of something new and then persuading them why it is right for them. Perhaps you are persuading people to join your company, or a bank to lend you more capital, or customers about a new product you'd like them to stock. The tendency here is to focus purely on rational arguments as a means of persuasion. As we have seen in various chapters previous to this, people don't buy purely on rational grounds – and the same goes for buying into the persuasive message of a presentation. So don't forget to appeal to the emotional side of your audience.

To entertain

Your objective may be to entertain. Being asked to be a best man at your friend's wedding, and therefore make the dreaded speech, which just has to be funny, is certainly one example of a presentation where the purpose is to entertain. However, in business, while you certainly want the audience to enjoy and remember your presentation, a best man type approach may not be professional or acceptable to some people. One danger is that people remember the jokes you tell rather than the message you were trying to get across. Please do not feel obliged to tell jokes if it doesn't come naturally to you – nothing is so embarrassing for you and the audience than a joke that doesn't come off.

Once the objective is clear you should consider the audience you will present to. As a result of your presentation what do you want them to *know, feel* and *do*?

Having sat through many a presentation, I sometimes come away feeling that the speaker intended to bore me to tears. They managed to get me into the room to listen in the first place – they wasted a prime opportunity to get me to leave that room knowing something new, feeling motivated and wanting to go back to work and share the information.

It will also be helpful at this early stage if you can get as much of an understanding of your audience as possible – especially if it is an external presentation you will be making.

- How many people will be present?
- What levels of experience do they have?
- How much background do they know?
- Will they understand industry jargon?
- Will decision makers be present?
- Who are they key people to get on your side?
- How much time do they have to spare?
- Do they feel positive or negative about the topic?

Clarify as much of this as you can. It will help enormously in deciding how much of your presentation needs to inform, persuade or entertain and what you want this audience to know, feel and do as a result.

Think of the presentation as a product you are selling and the audience as your potential customers. Your product must satisfy their needs – therefore you're going to have to tailor it accordingly if it is to have impact.

CONTENT/STRUCTURE

What's going to be in your presentation and how is it going to flow?

A simple way to think about the structure of your presentation is to compare it to the *News at 10*. Firstly the headlines tell you which reports to expect in the broadcast, then the broadcast itself details each report, and finally the closing couple of minutes summarises each of the reports. This traditional approach applies to any presentation.

Introduction – tell the audience what you're going to tell them
Body – tell them
Conclusion – tell them what you've told them

When working out exactly what you intend to say it's worth writing your conclusions first. If you had just three messages to get across, just three sentences to leave with you audience, then what would they be? Then, write down all the arguments or facts you need to make in order to support your conclusions. At this stage don't worry about the order of the facts. Once you have brain-stormed all the information you feel is relevant you can then go through it and look where the natural linkages and flow lies. Prioritise the information – it is not the time to show off how much you know, you need to present what will be relevant for the audience. Having done this you can prepare your introduction – by this stage you will know what you are going to talk about and why, so it will be easy to give a quick resumé of what the audience can expect.

Having considered the structure, let's look in more detail at the content of each element of your presentation.

Introduction

A strong introduction is really important. It grabs attention straight away – it tells the audience why it's going to be important for them to listen. This is your only opportunity to set the scene and control the presentation. Therefore tell people what you're going to cover, how long you're going to take and how you'll handle questions (at the end or as you're going through). If you anticipate that someone is expecting to hear about something you are not going to cover, tell them now – otherwise they'll spend the whole time waiting to hear that one thing and as a result hear nothing else you say.

Consider how you can use *hooks* to draw in an audience and hold their attention. Make it clear to the audience what the benefits are to them in listening. There are different types of hooks/benefits you could use:

■ opportunities	– let me show how we can improve branch sales by 15 per cent per month
	– this new working practice will give you much more flexibility in your working hours
■ fear	– unless we recruit an office manager, we are in danger of losing the best secretaries we have ever had
	– unless the VAT return is completed by the end of this quarter we face a fine which means we can't afford the incentive trips as promised
■ mystery	– a revelation which will intrigue the audience enough to hold their attention. Perhaps it could be a mysterious statement or the showing of an unusual object you constantly refer to, the meaning of which will become clear as you go on
■ show stoppers	– a startling or controversial statement such as 'We'll never grow any bigger or get any better' – and you go on to explain that other people are saying this, but let me show how I'm going to prove them wrong.

Body

The body of your presentation is the heart of the matter. You told them in the introduction that you were going to demonstrate five key benefits of your product or service. Or you told them that you were going to present the three pieces of activity that would drive your profit in the year ahead. The body provides the detail. And the problem with many 'bodies' is that the presenter and the audience get bogged down in the detail. The flow and logic become blurred, main messages get diluted and the presentation becomes less effective.

Think of the body as the route map to your destination. Start with topic A and link it to topic B which you can link to topic C and so on. Ensure the logic flows well. If you are on point three of six points you intend to make then tell the audience. This is called signposting. Signposts help your journey, they let the audience know where you are and keep everyone on track.

As the body will account for around 80–85 per cent of the length of any presentation it's important to pitch it right for the needs of the audience – draw them in as much as possible. Do this by:

- using real and relevant examples that they can relate to
- giving evidence to demonstrate and reinforce key points
- integrating the experience and expertise of key people
- using emotional as well as rational arguments
- asking them questions (be sure you know you will get the answer you want lest you be thrown off track!)
- using personal anecdotes.

There is a limit to the amount of data you can cram into the body of a presentation for it all to be remembered. If you have five key messages, make sure you use the strongest first and last. People will be alert at the start of the presentation and, if you signpost well, when you say 'and finally . . .' their ears are sure to prick up and listen intently to the final message. (Of course, get your voice and body language right and you can assume that the delivery of each and every one of your messages will be equally effective!)

Conclusion

Just as your introduction should grab the attention of everyone concerned, so to should your conclusion/summary be a powerful one. Finish on a weak note and people will remember the weakness rather than the validity of the arguments throughout. Often the ending of some books I read leave me disappointed – despite a great body or core story I close the cover and remember the bad ending rather than the strength of the story.

In a presentation the conclusion is intended to reiterate the key points and to leave a final clear message to the audience. They should go away in no doubt as to your objective – we need to buy this product, we need to get back to you within one week confirming new credit terms, this company is one to be taken seriously, this business is one that we definitely need to feature in our forthcoming article. The conclusion is not the time to throw in new important messages that you forgot to mention in the body.

Depending on your audience, your objectives and your confidence, you can consider differently structured approaches to the presentation. They all still follow the introduction, body and conclusion outline, but take slightly different routes. These different approaches are:

1. Classical
2. Pros and Cons
3. Persuasive

1. Classical

Introduction	Outline to follow	There are 3 key reasons to consider new windows.
Body	Reason 1	Firstly, they are long lasting and hardwearing.
	Recap reason 1 and mention reason 2	In addition to durability they come in a range of styles to suit any home: modern or traditional.

	Recap 1 and 2 and mention reason 3	As well as durability across a wide range of styles, we can offer immediate no mess fitting and disposal of your old windows.
Conclusion	Recap all 3 reasons	With these 3 benefits of . . . we can guarantee windows you will be pleased to recommend to any of your friends.

2. Pros and Cons

Introduction	Outline of the issue	You've been considering replacing the windows in your house. Let me tell you about what we can offer.
Body	Arguments for	Firstly, they are manufactured from extremely durable materials . . . (detail) Secondly, no matter the style of your house, our windows will not look out of place . . . (detail) Thirdly, you will add immediate value to the property . . .(detail)
	Summary of arguments for	So the benefits of replacing your windows are . . .

	Arguments against	However, it does require a fairly large initial outlay, it will require workmen in your home for several days, and there may be some noise and dust.
	Summary of arguments against	So, yes, there are 3 counter arguments . . .
Conclusion	View you take	However, having considered the arguments for and against new windows, on balance I hope you agree that the advantages outweigh the negatives.

3. Persuasive

Introduction	Outline of the purpose or problem	Have you ever had the problem of draughts and water coming in your windows?
Body	Reasons against	Now you could be saying that new windows are one of the most expensive outlays on your property, won't suit the style of your home, or that modern materials used are not as durable as traditional windows.
	Demolish reasons against	However, our windows could be the answer.

	Reasons for/ benefits	Manufactured from durable high-quality materials, they cut down on draughts and reduce the heating bills in your home. Available in styles to suit homes modern or traditional. The total cost is not as high as you may think.
Conclusion	Action or selling points	Please allow us to show you our range . . .

If you know your audience well, then you can choose the approach that will suit best.

DELIVERY

Remember that the manner in which you deliver, how you sound and how you look account for around 93 per cent of the effectiveness of any presentation. This may depend very much on your confidence, so you should take every opportunity you can to practise presenting. Ask people for some honest feedback on how you could do better, what you do well and less well. Ask them to focus not on the message but the delivery.

Using your voice

If you don't sound excited or enthusiastic when you speak, then why on earth should your audience be interested, excited or enthused by what you are saying – you are in danger of boring the audience to death. If you speak in a long, rambling monotonous drone, your audience will switch off.

If you want to enthuse people you must sound enthusiastic. If something is fantastic, stress it by sounding excited by it. When

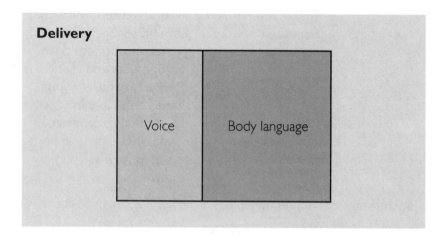

you want to get key points across you should emphasise them by varying the loudness or tone of your voice.

Pausing occasionally can have a powerful effect – it gathers back the attention of an audience who have drifted off, it gives people time to reflect on a dramatic statement you have made, it signals natural progression from one topic to another.

Beware of talking too quickly or too quietly (although speaking quietly on some occasions as a contrast can stress certain points).

You may have some habits you are not even aware of – if you can stand to, record yourself presenting and play the tape back. You may be surprised at the number of 'ums', 'ems', 'you know what I means'. I knew a very senior director in one company who had the unfortunate habit of clearing his throat constantly throughout every presentation. It was such a shame – I don't think anyone had ever told him. No one used to listen to a word he said – instead most people sat and counted the number of times it happened to see who had won the sweep that had been set up before his slot.

Using body language

Practise using your body, all of it, to look open and relaxed. It instils confidence in your audience be it large or small. There are five main considerations.

Firstly, smile – you may not feel like it, but it makes you look positive and such an attitude speaks volumes. It also encourages your audience to smile back, and sometimes there is nothing so reassuring while talking than seeing someone smiling along to what you are saying.

Secondly, look people in the eye. Don't stare at them until they feel intimidated, but make sure you are looking at the audience. You will need to be confident of the content of your message to ensure you don't talk down into pieces of paper and notes.

Thirdly, be aware of nervous gestures and mannerisms that people could lock on to – men in particular can be guilty of stuffing their hands into their trouser pockets (it's comforting I know) but when you start jingling with all the loose change in there it looks a little bizarre! So, if you put hands in pockets because you don't know what else to do with them, make sure your pockets are empty. Likewise beware repeatedly clicking the mechanism of a ballpoint pen you may be holding – it's so annoying. You may not know you run your hands through your hair or scratch your neck, so get some feedback – some gestures can give the impression that you are really uncomfortable or even lying – all of which will detract from your message.

Fourthly, we mentioned hands briefly in the previous paragraph, but to expand here, I don't think there are absolute rules as to what you do with them. Definitely don't put them over your mouth stifling your words. I think they can be used to great effect to reinforce important points or to gesture shapes, sizes and so forth. Should you be sitting to present to people across a table beware putting your hands behind your head too often. While it may indicate that you are relaxed it can come across as arrogance as opposed to confidence. Similarly when standing, hands on hips too often can come across as angry or defensive.

Fifthly, and finally, don't try to hide behind a desk or your equipment. People want to see you and hear you clearly and you don't need the feeling of restricted movement which comes from hiding – if you're feeling nervous hiding only intensifies the feeling of no escape!

During your delivery you may decide to use visuals to support you, so it's to this that our final area looks.

SUPPORTING MATERIAL/VISUALS

Think of the section above on delivery as one on 'Using yourself to create impact'. They are your natural aids to presenting. There is, of course, a whole suite of artificial aids at your disposal to also create impact.

Artificial/visual aids

- flipcharts
- overhead projectors/slides
- computer presentation
- props
- sales brochures/detail aids.

Artificial aids are not a substitute for natural aids – a slick and professional looking presentation delivered from a computer will not compensate for or detract from poor delivery.

The most important thing I want to say here is that you *do not need to use fancy Powerpoint/computer* techniques in presentations. There may be some instances where the professional image conveyed will be important, but you don't need a computer. Most people I have seen present using computers hide behind them. They get drawn into using fancy graphics, dreadful graphics, music, whooshing slogans flying in from all angles on screen, poor colours and far too much detail on each page. They rely totally on the screen doing the presentation rather than personally delivering it. Then the technology crashes and the presenter is left with nothing – they were so reliant on the technology that they have no idea what or how to present!

Why do you need to use artificial/visual aids?

- to help the audience (not prop up the presenter)
- reinforce key points
- add interest
- display complex figures and data
- demonstrations.

The reasons for using artificial and visual aids are summarised above. Therefore, please do not write every word you intend to say verbatim on a slide, computer screen or flipchart. All your audience need is a bulleted list of the key points which will help them follow the flow of the presentation.

If you are informing the audience of sales growth or profit projections or sharing potentially complex data, visual aids are essential. Using graphs or pie charts or bar graphs make it easy for the audience to capture the essence of the point.

Compare the visual aids below.

Both are supporting precisely the same piece of information, but it is easy to see that the chart is the more audience friendly – the presenter can verbally give the facts given as bullet points.

Bulleted form

Sales history

■ Sales have grown steadily every year for the past 3 years, at an average of 5% per year, but we have outperformed in the London region where sales last year grew 15%.
■ In the West region our sales have been falling steadily for the last 3 years.

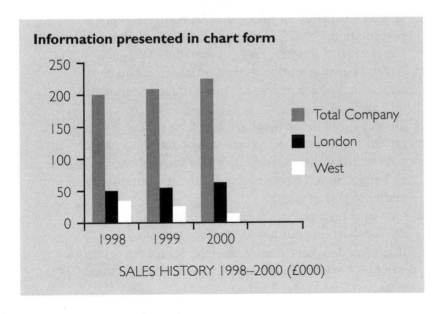

Information presented in chart form

SALES HISTORY 1998–2000 (£000)

Flipchart

Some tips for using flipcharts in your presentations are explained below.

- Great for capturing audience answers, suggestions, thoughts as you go through a presentation.
- Write big and bold in black or blue or any strong dark colour (red, yellow, light green, pink, etc. are fine for underlining and bullet point marks but difficult to read from a distance).
- If preparing sheets in advance to support each section of the presentation, do not write sentences – write bullet points only.
- Make the page big and bold – six bullet points should be fine, any more and the writing may be too small for all of the audience to see.
- If someone in the audience asks you to clarify a point or give more information you may want to use the flipchart to draw or write an explanation – therefore to save flipping back and forward and risk losing the place in your flipchart presentation, consider leaving some blank sheets between the pages of your pre-prepared presentation. It is good to do this in your preparation as well, as it means you have anticipated where people are likely to require more information.
- Do not speak to the flipchart. It will be beside or behind you, but do not be tempted to turn away from the audience – all your words will be absorbed, but by the flipchart and not the audience. So write on or refer to the flipchart, turn back to the audience and then talk.
- One final logistical tip. If you are right-handed, have the flipchart on your left as you face the audience. If left-handed, have it on your right. It enables you to write on it without covering and obscuring the entire page.

Overhead projector (OHP) tips

Many of the tips are similar to those for flipcharts:

- bullets rather than long sentences
- 6–8 lines maximum – not too much text
- beware small letters no one can read
- check the colours you use are legible.

There are other tips relevant only to OHPs:

- Acetates are great for showing crisp, clear graphs and charts or tables of figures – make it clear what they are demonstrating by giving each a title.
- Always, but always, test the OHP before using it – make sure it is in focus, the bulb works and the screen is clean.
- If your acetate has eight bullet points on it then perhaps you want to reveal each one as you provide the detail about it. By all means have a sheet of paper to cover up the points you haven't come to yet. The danger is that should someone open a door, or you sneeze, the sheet of paper may fly off revealing everything. Or perhaps the floor is not completely flat and the sheet of paper slides off unless held. A great tip here is to place the sheet of paper under the acetate – the weight of the acetate will hold it in place, and it means your next bullet points are visible to you as a prompt.

Props

I love props in presentations. It adds some interest to the conversation and brings the topic to life. Imagine going to buy a new car and having neither a picture of the model nor a model to see. What is the likelihood of you buying this car compared to the one which you could look at, sit in, touch and test drive? It's similar to a presentation – take as many examples of physical things along to demonstrate your point.

Sales presenters/detail aids

When making a presentation to customers with the purpose of selling or informing them of new products and services, a detail aid can be very useful, especially where you don't have samples to demonstrate. The detail aid may be a leave behind or not. Whichever, it should follow the rules and tips suggested above using and preparing visual aids.

- bullet point key features and benefits and the offer
- show pictures to break up the text
- show any complex or numerical data on charts
- plan carefully (based on the customer) the level of technical detail to show and on which to focus
- make it look as professional as possible.

If you feel the detail aid looks a professional and positive representation of your offer, you could not only use it on sales presentations, but mail it to prospects in advance of a meeting to stimulate their interest.

Finally, what about leaving behind a copy of your presentation? Well, I think that if it has been a formal presentation to customers, banks, etc. then, yes, you should leave something for the audience to refer back to. Bind together or place in a professional cover, a copy of your key points, perhaps the bullet points from the visual aids. There is no need to leave behind your words and notes word for word. People want a summary reminder.

Issue this summary at the end of the presentation rather than at the start, unless people specifically wish to write notes on the relevant pages as you are going through. But beware of them reading the document rather than listening to you.

And that is it – presentation over. Ready for the next one. Trust me, the more you do it the easier and easier it gets. The important skills of delivery and style start to become second nature leaving you time to worry about all the other little things you've got on your plate!

Reading the next chapter on motivating specific individuals will help you see which style of structure, which delivery style and which supporting material to adopt.

SUMMARY CHECKLIST

- Preparation is absolutely essential
- Use your natural ability – if you are not a natural comedian, do not feel that you need to tell jokes
- Be really clear what the purpose of the presentation is and who the audience are – how are they likely to be feeling and behaving?
- Grab attention or people will switch off
- Use hooks to draw in the audience
- Hold the interest and rouse desire by using examples, anecdotes and appealing to the emotion
- Remember you are your best visual aid.

12

How To Motivate People Around You

The greatest motivational act one person can do for another is to listen.
Ron E. Moody

THE CHAPTER AT A GLANCE

Business success depends on motivating customers to be loyal to you. But we often forget the need to keep the people around us motivated – staff, business partners, even yourself to enjoy the business you set up.

In early 2001 the *Sunday Times* published its guide to the '50 Best Companies to Work For' in Britain. The best companies all operate environments where people feel motivated and valued. You don't need to be a large company to aspire to that. Motivating people around you should never be seen as a chore.

This chapter looks at why motivation is important (not least because a happy working atmosphere makes your job as a small business owner a bit easier) and why people might not be motivated. It may be harder to motivate people in a small company than a large, and I look at the reasons why. Then I give some general tips to help motivate people, before moving on to look at specific motivations of individuals and different approaches to take in order to motivate them.

WHY MOTIVATED PEOPLE ARE IMPORTANT

- Represent the face of the company
- Form the first or last impression
- Differentiate your offer
- Improved performance

- Positive work atmosphere
- Self-fulfilment and preservation
- Staff retention.

It is a fact that people who are well motivated perform better than those who are not. And while I'm not sure if it's been proven to be, I am convinced that well motivated people make your business more successful.

Back in Chapter 8 we said that sometimes the staff provide the only opportunity to differentiate a company from its competition. I know that in my town there are three petrol stations and all else being the same (the price is always within 1p per litre of each other, they all sell newspapers and have a carwash), I always go to the one where the staff are at least pleasant. My assumption is that the reason they are pleasant is that they are motivated. Motivated staff provide better service to their customers. Better standards of service than the competition may encourage customer loyalty – a key driver of business performance.

My local pub has become my local pub simply by virtue of the staff – its competitive advantage is absolutely the way the staff treat the customers: they acknowledge me as a regular drinker (what a complimentary description!) and they are pleasant to be around. They are motivated staff.

And, of course, motivated staff who provide better service to their customers are also likely to provide better standards of performance for their employers or colleagues. The bar staff clean ashtrays regularly, empty bins, fill shelves with mixers, offer ice and sliced lemon in drinks, collect glasses, empty dishwashers and promptly serve customers. High standards in these areas which are important to the bar owners have a knock-on effect in driving customer service too – the bar looks cleaner, tables tidier, drinks more professional, stock readily available.

Now if the staff didn't enjoy their job, hated their boss and positively despised having to make small talk with a crowd of people who are in effect total strangers to them (i.e. were not motivated in their work), I'm not sure the pub would survive. Motivated staff are a real credit to the business – they represent the face of a business and could determine the success of it too.

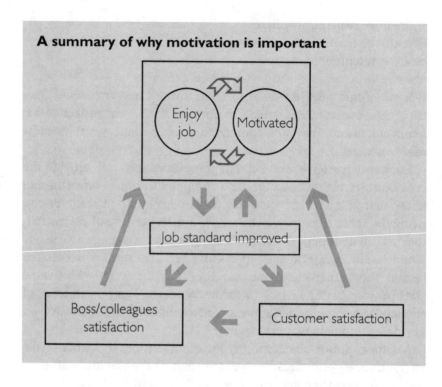

A summary of why motivation is important

People around you who enjoy their job, or are happy at work are motivated, and being motivated allows you to enjoy the job more. Such motivation enables people to do their job well – the job standards are improved. Improved job standards satisfy people around them at work and, of course, satisfy the customers, which in turn satisfies people at work. Happy bosses and colleagues hopefully give feedback to staff which can be a great motivator, and satisfied customers giving unprompted or prompted feedback drives motivation levels further. A worrying statistic, however, is that only 36 per cent of British workers are happy in their jobs (University of Warwick study).

You need motivated people around you if there is to be a happy working atmosphere. And you need motivated people around you if they are to come across as the professional and competent face of the company. In an environment where all of us are doing the jobs of more than one person, it's pretty hard to get through the week/day/month if you are not motivated. If you are getting no self-satisfaction then why continue? Don't forget that this may have been one of the reasons you set up your small business.

Unemployment is at its lowest level since 1975 and in today's job market a shortage of skilled workers is more of an issue than a shortage of jobs. Well-qualified workers can afford to be choosy. Many companies, small ones in particular are saying how difficult it is to get good people to work with. Not only are you going to have to try harder to attract them in the face of big companies with big benefits packages, but you are also going to have to try hard to keep them – motivate them or they'll leave!

Imagine the devastating effect lack of motivation can have – especially in a small business where people rely on each other so much to ease the burden of already heavy workloads. Consider, too, the one thing you will need as the owner of the small business to put things right – the one thing of which you have least – time.

Motivating the people around you should therefore never be seen as a chore, or as one of those management things you need to do once a week. Think of it as an on-going part of running your business – just as important as getting the price right, the communication right, the customer relationships right, the distribution policy right. If demotivated staff results in annoyed or unhappy customers then the greatest offer in the world will only be a short-term success. Motivation levels at the first and last points of contact with the company may determine the customer impression.

WHY MIGHT PEOPLE BE DEMOTIVATED AND HOW DO YOU TELL?

People who are not motivated or happy at work are likely to show poor performance: for themselves, for you, for customers and so for the business. This poor performance will be apparent in three key areas:

- reduced efficiency and productivity
- reduced customer satisfaction
- declining business results.

Specifically you are likely to experience all or some of the following:

■ being less punctual
■ increasing number of days absent through sickness
■ challenging of work guidelines without suggested improvements (being argumentative for the sake of it)
■ reducing care in on-the-job standards
■ doing the absolute minimum required and no more
■ complaining, but not to you, to colleagues
■ increasing customer complaints about staff.

You've got to understand why people around you might not be motivated. If you set up your business because of demotivation in your previous employment, remember what caused it and make sure you're not fostering the same resentments and causes. These reasons are summarised and explained below.

■ no belief in your offer
■ no source of help
■ lack of prospects
■ lack of rewards
■ unclear business purpose/direction
■ lack of influence in the business
■ unclear job description/expectations
■ boredom
■ lack of development opportunities
■ problems at home
■ life changes
■ not suited to the job
■ lack of example from above
■ inappropriate management style.

Perhaps your staff who have to sell or interact with customers have no belief in the offer. You may have 120 per cent belief in your product or service and understand in detail what it does, why it is better than all others like it and what are the real benefits the customer will gain. But do your people? Do they really? As a result, do they half-heartedly represent your offer? Are they unable to answer every question posed by customers, or unable to get access to someone who can answer? So do they go home each week feeling as though they have failed the company or the customer or themselves personally?

Do your staff feel as though they have prospects? Do they feel that they are doing something of value? Are they quite happy to come to work and do what they've always done, or do they want to move on and feel that they themselves are developing? Are there opportunities to develop their careers in your business?

Do people get rewarded? By this I don't mean do they get paid at the end of each week or month. Paying someone what they are owed for a job they have done should not be seen as a motivator, but the minimum standard. That's a bit like a supermarket saying that they will motivate customers to shop with them by offering free carrier bags. Free carriers are minimum standards needed to compete in the customers' eyes – they are certainly not motivators. The extras such as someone to pack your bags and carry them to your car may be the motivators. So what do we mean by rewarding them? Do they get recognition by their peers and the boss, praise from customers and management, thanks for a job well done? Do they actually feel valued? The biggest error is to assume that all rewards have to be financial ones.

Do your people know and understand what it is your business is trying to achieve? Do they know that you want to be the first choice among a certain segment of customers? Do they know that you see your key competitor as X and therefore everything has to be better than this benchmark? Do they know what you want to stand for? If your business plan and strategy is not well communicated to them, do not expect them to focus on the key areas of importance.

To build on this point, if your people do not feel that they can influence the direction of or ever make an impact on the business, they are unlikely to be motivated to do their work and your company justice. When I run training events for organisations then one of the major observations I witness and listen to is people's unhappiness in the belief that they can never make a difference to the way things are done. It seems bizarre that companies recruit people on the basis of their 'get up and go' and 'ability to take responsibility and drive change', yet within a year or so (and sometimes much sooner) those same people feel disillusioned and jaded when ideas are not listened to or even encouraged.

One reason for the jaded demotivation may be that the individual's job description is not clear. 'If I don't know what I'm meant to be doing how do I ever know if I'm doing it well or not?' 'If I'm not getting praise or recognition is it because I'm not doing my job as well as I should?' 'What do you really expect of me today/this week/this month?'

Linked still with this need for clarity around what your business is trying to achieve and what you expect of your people to help get there, is the principle of them understanding your business model. Imagine you only break even on a deal when selling at a price of £100. Do your people know this? Do they think it's just as good to have sold 10 at a price of £80 than 8 at a price of £100 this week? They finish the week flush with excitement at their achievements yet get no praise as in fact they've made a loss for the company.

Are they bored rigid doing the job? Have you read *Charlie and the Chocolate Factory* by Roald Dahl? I have vivid memories of Charlie's father who toils all day for a pittance of a wage in the local toothpaste factory, screwing lids on tubes of toothpaste. How did he manage to drag himself off to work every day? What kept him motivated at work? How did he alleviate the boredom of the repetitive tasks?

Are your people ever given the opportunity to learn something else? Are they ever trained formally or informally to learn new things which could help their sense of achievement and the business? Think about how you feel when you achieve or learn something new for the first time.

One thing you may need to consider as a cause of demotivation is a problem at home. Totally unwork-related issues do not disappear when that person enters the workplace, and can have a devastating effect on the usual efficiency and productivity of that person.

For the last few months our media has been bombarded with 'improvement' shows. Improve your looks, your hair, your home, your garden and now your life. People are consciously and subconsciously being asked to reevaluate their lives and the work/leisure balance. Many are opting out of the 'rat race' for a better quality of life, or at least asking themselves what they are doing with their life. It is unrealistic to expect such people at work to remain focused and motivated on their roles.

Let's be totally honest and admit that sometimes people are demotivated because they are just not suited to the job they do. If Lorraine loves speaking to people and gets a kick out of solving customers' problems, she is clearly going to be very unhappy working alone with no outside contact everyday. If Margaret hates using the telephone, then there is little value to you or her in making her a telephone salesperson charged with generating 50 calls per day.

Your staff have been quite clearly briefed on how to deal with customers, how to handle the returns policy, working hours, dress code, etc. – all the basics you have put in place for your business. Now imagine how they feel when you come in and totally contradict all of these basics. Yes, you may be the boss and, as they probably appreciate, can do exactly as you please, but don't expect your staff to remain motivated if you refuse to lead by example.

Now imagine I am a kind and sensitive soul who likes to have things explained to them – what I'm expected to do and why I'm being asked to do it and how it will benefit everyone. Now imagine my manager never explains such things – just do this Lynn by Friday would you? No time to explain. And it's not one-off behaviour; he's always like this. How motivated do you think I feel when the management style is inappropriate?

How do you feel after reading this chapter so far? Not too motivated I'd bet. And that's the reality of motivation. Even negative talk and atmospheres can spiral – something that was a small and easy to resolve issue could escalate into a serious motivation problem. Recognise the symptoms early. Don't see motivation as something you need to do as a quick fix or extra management task – it should be built in to your work practices. Be aware that everything you do as a company should motivate your employees and colleagues just as much as your customers.

MOTIVATING IN SMALL AND LARGE BUSINESSES

There are many reasons why motivation is easier in a small business than in a large organisation, but unfortunately one or two large reasons why it is more difficult.

Why is motivation easier in a small company?

■ people can see what you are trying to achieve as a business and potentially feel more a part of it and a contribution to that success

■ they feel that they can really influence the direction of the business

■ senior management are much closer to the business – they are less likely to be perceived as out of touch with the customer-facing frontline

■ it is easy for them to see the effects, quickly, after implementation of one of their ideas

■ it is easier for a company of 10 to celebrate success than for a company of 500

■ you are close to the individuals, close enough to gauge their unique motivations and act on them

■ there are no rigid procedures that say you can't give Mary a pay rise because all the others at her level would be miffed.

Why is motivation difficult in a small company?

■ getting a job promotion is motivational, but in a small company level upon level of management is unlikely to be present and therefore promotional opportunities are limited, so there are problems in promoting and satisfying long-term aspirations of individuals

■ negativity can spread immensely quickly as the effects of one person's demotivation can have a strong and adverse impact on colleagues

■ if your staff have come from a large organisation, they may find
it difficult to adapt to the perceived lack of structure and fixed
career development guidelines. In a large company it is
relatively easy to gauge your performance by saying that in
18 months I should be a senior sales executive, and after
24 months a sales manager, etc.

GENERAL TIPS TO MOTIVATE PEOPLE

1. *Encourage belief in your offer.* Ensure that those representing
   your offer externally really believe in it – what it is, what it
   does, why it is better, what are the benefits. Train them to
   ensure they understand the product or service and can
   anticipate any questioning by a customer.
2. *Support network.* Have someone on hand for people to refer
   to, ask questions of, and receive guidance and support.
3. *Opportunities to develop.* Demonstrate that you are concerned
   about their development – either through promotion or on-
   the-job training and coaching of new skills.
4. *Reward people.* Financial or non-financial, celebrate their
   successes, praise them, recognise their achievements, respect
   their work, share good news for others to learn from.
5. *Value every contribution.* Convince people that every
   contribution they make is valued. Encourage them to feel
   pride in their achievements.
6. *Sympathy to personal problems.* Never ignore the existence of a
   life outside of work. Humanity in times of illness or personal
   tragedy can steer people through work and remain as positive
   as humanly possible. It can count for much when things
   return to normal.
7. *Be an inspiring leader.* Successful, dynamic, charismatic
   leaders can drive and motivate a workforce. Carphone
   Warehouse and Pret a Manger began as small businesses
   and are now hugely successful organisations under the
   same leadership as at their start. Tom Farmer was an
   inspiring leader who took Kwik Fit on to great
   things.

8. *Share the vision.* Something a successful leader will do is share the vision of the business. Everyone knows the direction the business is taking, what the business is trying to achieve and why. Everyone knows what the vision means to them as an individual in the business.

9. *Clarify job descriptions.* Having a shared and relevant vision and big picture of the business will ensure everyone knows why they are doing what they are doing. But individuals day-to-day also need to know exactly what is expected of them, what defines excellent performance and so on. Clarify this and reduce misunderstandings.

10. *Set a good example.* One thing that marks an inspiring leader is one who 'walks the talk'. Be seen to act in the way you'd like motivated staff to behave and you're certainly on the road to motivation.

11. *Welcome and use suggestions.* Firstly, welcome suggestions and then make sure you listen to them. Value their contributions. If you then go on to action someone's suggestion then great – but make sure you don't pass it off as your own – recognise and reward the suggestions of others. It's an immediate way to motivate others to involve themselves in the future direction of your business.

12. *Clarify parameters.* If you don't want to particularly sell to one customer, as you know he's a credit risk, make sure everyone knows. Define the parameters of good business practice.

13. *Alleviate boredom.* You can't help some tasks required at work being less than cerebrally challenging – in fact, being downright boring. Can you share them around? Can you encourage competition to alleviate the boredom? For example, can you screw the tops on 100 tubes faster than last week?

14. *Right person doing right job.* Try to match the personality to the job. You have only yourself to blame if you get this wrong. It means you have to be rigorous during the recruitment phase to ensure you get the right kind of person for each task.

15. *Communicate properly.* Having all the characteristics of an inspiring leader is a help, but specifically you must also communicate in the right manner to each person. This has

been partly covered in the previous chapter on presenting your ideas, but will be explained more fully later in this chapter.

WHAT DETERMINES MOTIVATION?

Whether or not someone is motivated may be easy to see by his or her behaviour. However, what determines whether he or she is motivated is determined by many unseen factors: beliefs, values, ambitions, experiences, prejudices, perceptions, hopes, fears, stage in life, personal circumstances and so on. And these factors can change over time. What motivated someone last month may not motivate them next month. What motivates me is unlikely to be identical to that which motivates my friends. One job may motivate me while a completely different one may motivate my colleagues.

Just as your customers have unique needs and wants, so too do your company colleagues. Just as you try to satisfy the needs and

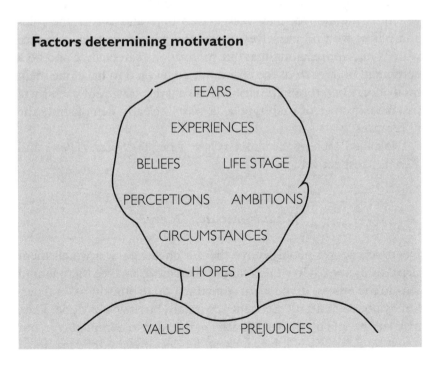

Factors determining motivation

FEARS

EXPERIENCES

BELIEFS   LIFE STAGE

PERCEPTIONS   AMBITIONS

CIRCUMSTANCES

HOPES

VALUES   PREJUDICES

wants of your customers through your offer, so too must you aim to satisfy the needs, wants and motivations of your colleagues.

We looked earlier at some general techniques for motivating people. Now we'll consider more specific ways to motivate different types of individuals.

INDIVIDUAL MOTIVATIONS

Just as you can group customers' requirements into clusters or segments, then so too can you group your staff motivations. While acknowledging that each of us is different, you can broadly classify the motivators of people as follows:

- the need to succeed/win and be seen to succeed
- the need to be liked by others and be asked to help others
- the need to be 100 per cent accurate/be right.

Each of us is motivated by one or a combination of the above, which as mentioned, may vary across time and across the roles and places we find ourselves in and the people we find ourselves with. While appreciating that our motivations can change and be a combination of each of the above, we do all tend to have one main motivator. Therefore in describing the characteristics of each I will use the extremes of each type as a way to clearly demonstrate the differences.

I've called each of the above types of person *Doers*, *Helpers* and *Thinkers* respectively.

What motivates Doers?

Doers are action people. Give them a challenge and watch them strive to succeed. Give them targets to achieve and see them aim to out-do the others. If you want something done quickly, ask a Doer. It may not be done 100 per cent accurately, but it will be done. They may rub people up the wrong way on the road to completing it, but it will be done. They'll be quickest, loudest, most confident, most successful and best – in their eyes. They think helpers are weak and wet and thinkers are slow and boring. Doers will be bored of this chapter now and will be onto the summary to find the quick fix answers on motivating people. (OK, I'm getting to the point!)

How to motivate a Doer

- give them challenging tasks to complete
- reward them publicly with praise, or give prizes (even token gestures)
- make everything measurable so they can easily identify how well they are doing or how much they need to do
- get to the point when communicating with them
- tell them what's in it for them
- be a dynamic leader
- welcome and encourage their feedback and suggestions
- allow them to come up with innovative ideas
- let them take decisions
- let them be in charge
- make things competitive.

How to demotivate a Doer

- indecision
- impossible goals
- long routine
- no competition
- no public recognition
- no control of resources/insufficient resources.

What motivates Helpers?

If anyone has a problem at work you can guarantee that the Helper has spotted it already – they'll be there offering condolence and assistance. The Helper needs to know that everything at work is

OK. They need reassurance that everyone is happy and content. They hate friction and tension and lack of consideration for others. They see Doers as arrogant and bossy and Thinkers as withdrawn loners. 'Why can't everyone just get along?'

How to motivate a Helper

- ensure the office environment is warm and welcoming
- ask them to mentor people having difficulties
- make sure you know personal details about them and recognise those details
- ask for their help
- make sure they're OK
- show feeling and concern for welfare of people
- show and appreciate how well everyone is getting on.

How to demotivate a Helper

- personal criticism
- betrayal
- selfishness
- a non-supportive work environment
- having to give instructions
- aggressiveness
- working alone.

What motivates a Thinker?

If you have a pile of data that requires analysis to find the completely right answer to a problem, Thinkers are the ones for the job. If you need someone to take all emotion out of the task and just get on and do the job right, pick a Thinker. They are really independent workers who like time to consider things logically and come up with the right answer. It may take a long time to get the right answer, but you can be sure it will be right. You may only have wanted a quick summary of the issue, but a Thinker will make sure they provide all 52 pages of background fact to explain their thinking in the matter. They see Helpers as interfering busybodies and Doers as risky show-offs.

How to motivate a Thinker

- don't rush them by giving them tight deadlines
- allow them the opportunity to reach their own conclusions
- ask them for reasons and suggestions
- giving accurate time scales to work with
- allowing them to work with factual data
- let them use their own initiative
- give them clear objectives
- show that you have planned ahead.

How to demotivate a Thinker

- substandard results
- not taken seriously
- deadline driven
- light-hearted work environment
- too teamy
- superficial decisions.

By considering the general motivation techniques, and now the more specific suggestions, we should have a pretty good idea about how to approach motivation among people around you.

There are three areas (see diagram on p. 232) that may motivate people:

- the actual job you are asking them to do
- the working environment they are in
- you and your style of management.

All three pillars are required if you are to motivate people – the process fails without the support of each.

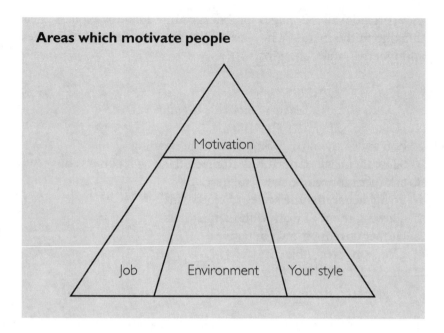

Areas which motivate people

The job and the environment we have more or less covered within the previous pages. For example, job approaches to motivation include:

■ don't get a Helper doing a Doer's job, or a Doer doing a Thinker's job and so forth
■ make sure the job guidelines and standards and expectations are crystal clear.

Environment approaches to motivation include:

■ providing comforts for your staff (tea, coffee and biscuits)
■ celebrating success
■ praising, recognising, valuing and rewarding
■ consulting people on important aspects of their role.

The remainder of the chapter is dedicated to the third element – you and your management style.

YOU AND YOUR MANAGEMENT STYLE

Think about your management style and what you are good at. If you're brave, ask some colleagues or partners for some feedback. Think, too, about the strengths and weaknesses of your style: the implications of your style on the people around you. For example, you may be very easy-going which many people will like; it makes you really approachable. But on the negative side perhaps this means you never make it clear absolutely what you want from everyone. Now consider how this affects the motivation of people around you. Try to be rigorous at this stage – take time to consider in detail your strengths and weaknesses and their implications on motivation.

All of us have a preferred style of communicating with others. You have been considering the strengths and weaknesses of this style. What is right with some people at some times may be inappropriate and ineffective at others. Just as the chapter on presenting your ideas showed, occasionally it may be the delivery rather then the message that determines successful motivation.

Imposing your usual style may demotivate. A Doer will switch off instantly if his or her manager adopts a Thinker approach that is slow, methodical, logical, rigorous and thorough. To be successful you must adapt your style to that of the person you are dealing with. Speak like a Helper when dealing with a Helper, like a Doer when dealing with a Doer, and a Thinker when dealing with a Thinker. Just beware insincerity, which people can spot a mile away.

MANAGEMENT/COMMUNICATION STYLE

If you were to consider the extremes of style of communicating with people, the arrow in the diagram on p. 234 shows that you have straightforward, prescriptive 'Telling' at one extreme and involving 'Delegating' at the other. Then, of course, you have all the variances in between, with the main style there being one that is participative and 'Consulting'.

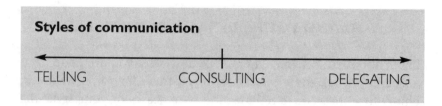

Telling

The emphasis in this style is very much about directing or instructing to ensure that the task is performed to an acceptable standard. There is little if any input from the individual being 'told'.

Consulting

This style revolves around providing guidance, support and encouraging the individual to take responsibility for their work achievements.

Delegating

Here your role is about letting the individual get on with the task in hand, and providing a broad outline of detail they will need in order to successfully complete the work.

Accepting that there are different styles, the critical issue is using the one that is appropriate to the situation and the individual in question. You will need to consider:

- level of motivation and willingness to do the job
- knowledge and ability to do the job
- confidence and experience of the job.

Where do you sit on the arrow? Do you change where you sit on different occasions? Which occasions? Are you using the right style at the right time with the right person?

When a communication style is appropriate

Style	When appropriate?
Telling	■ individual is new ■ individual has little or no experience of the task ■ no self motivation ■ lacks confidence ■ performing well below standard
Consulting	■ individual is skilled ■ variable motivation ■ performing above standard ■ will take responsibility for the task
Delegating	■ individual has skills, knowledge and experience ■ self-motivated and confident ■ initiates action

Imagine someone new joins your business. They've never worked in a small company before; perhaps they're new back to work after some time off. In this instance delegation or consultation would not be the most effective style to use. They're probably desperate for some direction: do's, don'ts, where to find what and who to speak to type of information. They need and want to be told certain things. It will make them feel comfortable and motivated to get on with their job.

Compared to consulting and delegating, telling certainly takes least time – someone asks you for help and you tell them what to do. However, for some people around you, telling would have a detrimental effect on their motivation. Surveys suggest that (no doubt partly due to time pressures on businesses) that 80 per cent of the time managers use a prescriptive telling style with people around. As a result people keep doing the same things in the same way, individuals begin to feel disempowered, they stop thinking for themselves and await orders, and then management resent these people who don't think for themselves. No wonder workplaces can be full of demotivated people – bosses and staff.

Consulting and delegating may take longer in the short term, but I guarantee they will work to your long-term advantage – both in terms of your time and your people development and motivation.

Imagine someone asks for help or you have something you'd like them to work on specifically and take responsibility for. Rather than telling them what to do, why not ask them what they think they should do? Ask them to get back to you with suggestions. Work together to come up with options. Challenge their suggestions and ask how they will work or could be improved. Ask questions to draw out their thinking and ideas. Listen carefully to their suggestions. Whichever option you end up going with, yours, theirs or a combination, this consulting style will help the individual, and certainly will motivate them:

- they may have learnt something new and so been helped with their development
- you have involved them and made them feel valued
- they may now be more confident to make more suggestions to you
- they may start to think through solutions rather than immediately coming to you with problems
- it may improve the relationship between you (which motivates both of you)

Failing to consult with someone who feels that they have the ability to contribute but is constantly being spoon fed and ordered around is the quickest way to demotivate skilled, enthusiastic people.

With delegating the motivation benefits are similar. However, in failing to delegate to those who are keen, the effect on their motivation levels are even more serious. In delegation, you are allowing the individual even more free rein to own the task. Ensure the objective of the task is clear and the targets agreed and understood. Set any boundaries (for example the maximum time or budget they have) and agree when you will meet to review progress. Then give them space and authority to get on with it.

SUMMARY CHECKLIST

- Find out why your people may be motivated or not – observe people at work and listen to the grapevine
- Ensure general approaches to motivation are in place

- Try to group the people around you into one of the three categories – Doer, Helper or Thinker
- Apply the specific techniques for motivation to these individuals
- Ensure you have considered the methods of motivation in terms of the job, the environment and your management style
- Be flexible – use different approaches with different individuals
- Telling, consulting and delegating communication styles will work to motivate different people at different times.

13
Places to Go for Help

*Feed a man a fish, feed him for a day,
teach a man to fish and feed him for life*

FOR ALL ROUND GOOD
ADVICE FOR SMALL BUSINESSES

1. *Business Links*. Local partnerships which bring together the
   services of chambers of commerce, local authorities, training
   and enterprise councils and other local bodies. Provide advice
   in all areas from putting together a business plan to finding
   accountants.
   www.businesslink.co.uk
   Telephone UK: 0845 756 7765
   Business Connect Wales: 0845 796 9798
   LEDU Northern Ireland: 028 9049 1031
   Scottish Business Shops: 0800 787878

2. *Department of Trade and Industry*. Get a copy of a great booklet
   called 'A Guide to Help for Small Business'. It details
   everywhere you could go for every type of assistance and
   advice.
   www.dti.gov.uk
   Telephone: 0870 1502 500

3. In Scotland contact *Scottish Enterprise Network* and their Small
   Business Gateway services. They provide information on
   everything from business start-up information to identifying
   new markets at home and abroad, advice on growth from a
   small team of professionals who have themselves launched and
   grown successful businesses, and help in drawing up growth
   action plans.
   www.sbgateway.com
   Telephone: 0845 609 6611

4. *Alodis* magazine for self-employed professionals. Launched March 2001 and covers all areas of working for yourself in a small business.
   ww.alodis.com
   Telephone: 020 7959 3011

5. *Starting your own Small Business* magazine, published by Crimson Publishing. Find them at:
   www.startups.co.uk

6. Other good government websites are:
   www.enterprisezone.org.uk – for links to different information
   www.up-and-running.co.uk – for general help
   www.companies-house.gov.uk – for booklets and company information

7. Information, advice on VAT, tax, Internet, franchising and, of course, communication as it is from BT, comes in *GetStarted*.
   www.bt.com/getstarted

8. *Usecolor.com* is a company who offers every service imaginable for the small business for a monthly fee – free legal advice, on line experts, purchasing assistance, IT help, finance and tax advice, and general advice and information you can download.
   www.usecolor.com
   Telephone: 0870 165 2009

FOR GOOD E-BUSINESS/INTERNET ADVICE

1. For help on anything to do with e-commerce speak to *UK Online for Business*.
   www.ukonlineforbusiness.gov.uk
   Telephone: 0845 715 2000

2. www.tradeuk.com is a Department of Trade and Industry site which is full of advice for anyone looking at international e-business who may have currency concerns.

3. Information, tools, services and advice to help you maximise the potential of the internet can be found at www.clearlybusiness.com. It is a venture between Freeserve and Barclays Bank, containing free guides and extra help for registered paid-up members. Also contains a wealth of advice on general small business matters, market information, local seminars and events, forums and discussion boards.

4. ebiz.co.uk run half-day seminars on web sites as business tools – how to get people to your site and keep them coming back www.ebiz.co.uk
   Telephone: 0800 018 5530

FOR GOOD ADVICE ON STAFF AND MOTIVATION

The *DTI* produces an information pack called 'Partnerships with People' (PWP). It gives models of good practice aimed at helping companies become better places to work. The PWP programme includes a fund available to help businesses mount improvement projects. Write to:
   The Department of Trade and Industry
   Admail 528
   London SW1 8YT
   or fax on 0870 150 2333

FOR PRESENTATION SKILLS

International Training in Communication (ITC) is a global organization and a registered charity, and have clubs throughout the UK who typically meet in the evening twice a month. The aim is the personal development of individuals through improved public speaking, presentation and other related communication skills. They operate at regional level. The national website is still under development. However, why not look at what one region have to offer as an example – they could help you contact your local ITC.
   http://members.tripod.co.uk/cheshcommitc/index.htm

FOR PUBLIC RELATIONS

1. The *Institute of Public Relations* offer a service called Matchmakers where for a fee they will recommend six PR specialists in your area.
Telephone: 020 7253 5151

2. The *PR Consultants Association* offers a similar service and booklets on finding the right PR people to use.
Telephone: 020 7233 6026

FOR SALES PROMOTIONS

For guidelines on the legality of any promotional offers, coupons or competitions you are considering contact the *Institute of Sales Promotion*:
Arena House
66–88 Pentonville Road
London N1 9HS
Telephone: 020 7837 5340

FOR LISTS OF PROSPECT CUSTOMERS

1. Try the 'Business Database' – part of *Yellow Pages*.
Telephone: 01753 212093
Database.Services@yellowpages.co.uk

2. Have a look in the weekly publication *Marketing Week* (on sale every Thursday) for a full listing of all agencies offering lists for sale or rent.

3. *HLB Ltd* claim to be the UK's leading end customer list broker and manager.
Telephone: 020 7243 8500

4. The *Royal Mail* are also worth contacting for information in this area.

Summary – Staying Ahead of the Game

1. Is there really a need for what you have to offer or are you doing it because you think it's a good idea?
2. Stay close to your key customers in a way that large companies find it hard to do.
3. 80 per cent of your business is likely to come from 20 per cent of your customers – make sure you stay close to them and keep them completely satisfied.
4. Be really clear why customers will buy from you rather than your competitors – what benefits are you offering customers that they can't get elsewhere?
5. Be clear about which customer needs you are satisfying – if you try to be all things to all people then you'll end up pleasing no one.
6. Don't put yourself at a disadvantage by competing without the skills and resources needed to satisfy customers profitably.
7. Make sure everyone who works for you and with you clearly understands that everything you do is about satisfying customers.
8. Remember what annoys you about being a customer and dealing with your suppliers – make sure your customers don't feel the same in dealing with you.
9. Know what you want to stand for in the mind of the customer and let it drive everything you do.
10. Loyal customers are the best advocates for your business.
11. Bad service is the main reason customers leave – much more than price.

12. Keep hold of current customers – it costs seven times as much to win back lost customers and four times as much to win new ones as it does to keep your existing customers.
13. Unhappy customers will leave, not tell you why and tell 9–13 friends not to deal with you.
14. Don't set your prices too low – it is very hard to put them up later.
15. Constantly monitor your environment to ensure your offer is still competitive and satisfying customers.
16. Know your strengths and weaknesses.
17. Consider the key opportunities and threats in your business environment and plan how to deal with them.
18. Live up to all your promises – if you must then underpromise and overdeliver – never underdeliver.
19. Know your competitors inside out.
20. Know how important you are to your customers and your suppliers.

References

Chapter 1
1. Philip Kotler, *Marketing Management:Analysis, Planning and Control*, Prentice-Hall, Hemel Hempstead, 1995.
2. Hugh Davidson, *Even More Offensive Marketing*, Penguin, Harmondsworth, 1997.

Chapter 5
1. Scott Adams, *The Dilbert Principle*, Boxtree, Basingstoke, 1995.

Chapter 8
1. Jan Carlson and Tom Peters, *Moments of Truth*, Harper Collins, London, 1989.

Chapter 9
1. Don Peppers and Martha Rogers, *The One-to-One Future*, Piatkus Books, London, 1993.
2. B. Joseph Pine II, Don Peppers and Martha Rogers, 'Do you want to keep customers forever?', *Harvard Business Review*, March/April 1995.
3. *op. cit.*
4. *op. cit.*

Chapter 10
1. Angus J. Kennedy, *The Internet Rough Guide 2000*, Penguin, Harmondsworth, 2000.

Index